Library as Safe Haven

Disaster Planning, Response, and Recovery

A How-To-Do-It Manual for Librarians®

Deborah D. Halsted
Shari Clifton
Daniel T. Wilson

Neal-Schuman
An imprint of the American Library Association

Chicago   2014

Printed in the United States of America
18 17 16 15 14   5 4 3 2 1

Extensive effort has gone into ensuring the reliability of the information in this book; however, the publisher makes no warranty, express or implied, with respect to the material contained herein.

ISBNs: 978-1-55570-913-6 (paper); 978-1-55570-949-5 (PDF); 978-1-55570-973-0 (ePub); 978-1-55570-974-7 (Kindle).

Library of Congress Cataloging-in-Publication Data
Halsted, Deborah D.
   Library as safe haven : disaster planning, response, and recovery : a how-to-do-it manual for librarians / Deborah D. Halsted, Shari Clifton, Daniel T. Wilson. — First edition.
      pages cm
   Includes bibliographical references and index.
   ISBN 978-1-55570-913-6 (alk. paper)
1. Libraries—Safety measures—Handbooks, manuals, etc. 2. Library materials—Conservation and restoration—Handbooks, manuals, etc. 3. Emergency management—Handbooks, manuals, etc. 4. Library planning—Handbooks, manuals, etc. I. Clifton, Shari. II. Wilson, Daniel T. III. Title. IV. Title: Disaster planning, response, and recovery : a how-to-do-it manual for librarians.
   Z679.7.H355 2014
   025.8'4—dc23
                                                            2014004669

♾ This paper meets the requirements of ANSI/NISO Z39.48-1992 (Permanence of Paper).

Contents

LIST OF ILLUSTRATIONS — vii

PREFACE — ix

Chapter 1. Risk Assessment and Continuity of Operations Plans — 1
Steps in Risk Assessment — 5
Conclusion — 15
References — 15

Chapter 2. Responding to a Threat — 17
The Importance of Immediate Responses — 18
Planning Responses Based on Potential Risks — 19
Designing Drills to Assist in Training for Response — 27
After-Action Review — 29
Conclusion — 29
References — 32

Chapter 3. From Self-Reliance to Asking for Help — 33
On-Site Planning — 34
Off-Site Planning — 38
Outside Assistance Planning — 39
Conclusion — 45
References — 45

Chapter 4. A One-Page Service Continuity Plan — 47
Background — 49
Service Continuity Pocket Response Plan — 50
Conclusion — 58
References — 58

Chapter 5. Tapping the Potential of Mobile Technologies and Social Media for Preparedness and Response ... 59

Mobile Technologies ... 59

Social Networking ... 61

Other Tools ... 63

Challenges ... 65

Conclusion ... 66

References ... 67

Chapter 6. Personal Preparedness and Possible Impact on Library Services ... 69

Create a Kit ... 69

Make a Plan ... 73

Specific Threats ... 74

Conclusion ... 89

References ... 89

Chapter 7. Leveraging the Library ... 91

Traditional Roles ... 92

Nontraditional Roles ... 96

Conclusion ... 102

References ... 102

Chapter 8. Two Model Scenarios for Cooperative Engagement ... 103

Hurricane Jenny ... 104

The Marshall City Earthquake ... 108

Conclusion ... 112

References ... 112

APPENDIX: RESOURCES ... 115

ABOUT THE AUTHORS ... 133

INDEX ... 135

Illustrations

Figures

Figure 2.1 Emergency Management Cycle 17

Figure 3.1 Memorandum of Understanding Relating to
Core Resources and Services Following a Disaster 40

Figure 4.1 Front Side of SCPReP 52

Figure 4.2 Back Side of SCPReP 53

Figure 4.3 Mobile SCPReP 54

Figure 4.4 SCPReP with Prepaid Phone Card 54

Tables

Table 1.1 Possible Events Causing Service Interruption 4

Table 1.2 Outside Experts 8

Table 1.3 Vulnerability Table for Houston, Texas 11

Table 2.1 Pandemic Planning: Stages of Pandemic and
Library Procedures 22

Table 2.2 Emergency Response Table 30

Preface

Since Hurricane Katrina devastated the Gulf Coast, librarians have become more involved with disaster preparedness and response activities in their communities and parent institutions. As library networks and associations, such as the National Network of Libraries of Medicine (NN/LM), the Medical Library Association (MLA), and the American Library Association (ALA), promote greater awareness and create training programs and resources, and as legislation, such as the Stafford Act, affirms the value of libraries in disaster response, much progress has been made. Still, many opportunities and roles continue to be underutilized or unexplored.

Library as Safe Haven: Disaster Planning, Response, and Recovery offers the reader a guide for exploring opportunities and developing new roles. Utilizing a model that focuses on continuity of core resources and services while enhancing the library's role through partnering with emergency planners, it is designed primarily for libraries; however, the content and resources contained within can easily be adapted to any business or agency in search of a well-structured approach to readiness and disaster response.

Organization of This Book

The first step in any disaster or Continuity of Operations (COOP) plan is that of risk assessment. Chapter 1, "Risk Assessment and Continuity of Operations Plans," discusses the steps in risk assessment, including creating a planning team; identifying possible hazards; conducting a vulnerability analysis; analyzing current strengths and weaknesses; inventorying assets and estimating potential losses; conducting an insurance assessment; considering mitigation options; and, finally, reviewing and updating the assessment. This chapter offers practical advice about the importance of conducting a risk assessment and how to complete the process, including whom to include on the team and what outside sources should be contacted. Table 1.3 (p. 11) offers a valuable vulnerability model that can be adapted to any geographic location.

Chapter 2, "Responding to a Threat," begins the discussion on how to respond to threats, especially emphasizing the importance of having trained staff on-site anytime the library is open. The ability to respond to threats must be based on knowledge of how to respond to specific threats that are identified in the results of the risk assessment conducted in the first step of disaster planning. This chapter also offers readers advice on designing drills to match the potential threats for a particular geographic area.

Chapter 3, "From Self-Reliance to Asking for Help," is designed to provide a background and structure for three important elements of disaster planning, including on-site planning, off-site planning, and obtaining outside assistance. Gaining knowledge of these three elements is essential in disaster planning and requires accurate documentation and diligent updating. It is important to be self-sufficient so that the library can respond effectively to small disasters, but, in the case of a major event, it is equally important to have plans in place to seek outside assistance from the parent institution, community, state, or even federal government.

Writing a complete disaster plan is initially a time-consuming task and becomes even more so with the necessary constant updating. Few library managers have time to devote to these tasks. Therefore, chapter 4, "A One-Page Service Continuity Plan," offers advice on a valuable plan adapted from a model created by the Council of State Archivists (CoSA), which makes developing and maintaining disaster and COOP planning much easier. This template is not copyrighted (CoSA just asks for everyone to acknowledge its authorship) and is adaptable to any size institution. The plan conveniently folds into a size that will fit any wallet so that it is easily accessible from anywhere. The plan can also be loaded onto a mobile device, which makes it even more portable. If a librarian is not able to create an extensive disaster plan, the CoSA template offers an excellent alternative.

It is clear that mobile technologies and social media have become ubiquitous in all aspects of today's society. While these applications have been used for many things, especially instant connectivity with large groups of people, it is easy to see how they can also be used in disaster planning. Chapter 5, "Tapping the Potential of Mobile Technologies and Social Media for Preparedness and Response," offers important tips on how to utilize social media and mobile technologies for a variety of devices and smartphones. The availability and use of these devices support the integration of a "whole community" approach, which is similar to the 1980s' concept of "It takes a village."

When a disaster strikes there is a great need for all staff to be available to assist with the response. Unfortunately, key staff may not be present because of the impact of the disaster at home. This means that, as part of the library's disaster planning, it is vital to ensure that staff members also have personal plans in place. Chapter 6, "Personal Preparedness and Possible Impact on Library Services," offers advice on creating a family disaster kit and how to respond to specific types of disasters. It also includes valuable vignettes from librarians who have experienced widespread disasters and how these disasters affected library services. Embedded in these stories is the common theme that librarians are dedicated to the library and to the continuity of services.

In the worst-case scenario, a disaster might eliminate the possibility of "normal" library services. Chapter 7, "Leveraging the Library," offers librarians a number of possible alternatives for standard library services. With preplanning and some specialized training, librarians can be in advantageous positions to prove their worth by stepping in and doing things that are not normally considered standard. Many of these tasks are just a slight deviation from what librarians already do, especially in the case of information dissemination. Additionally, through National Incident Management System, Incident Command System, and Community Emergency Response Team training, librarians can increase their role in community response to any event.

There are two basic categories of disasters, those which allow time for preplanning, such as a hurricane, and those which strike without notice, such as an earthquake. Chapter 8, "Two Model Scenarios for Cooperative Engagement," offers the reader fictional scenarios about how a library can plan for and respond to both an expected disaster and one that strikes without notice. As is mentioned in the chapter title, these scenarios highlight interagency cooperation. Librarians offer valuable knowledge and resources that not only can help restore library services but also can be a vital key in community response and recovery.

The book closes with an appendix that is rich with resources to help librarians through all stages of a disaster—before, during, and after. The websites focus on nonprofit, commercial, and government resources and on resources that support mobile technologies.

Ideally, no librarian would ever have to face a disastrous situation, but the reality is that many will. Every geographic area of the world faces environmental challenges, be it a hurricane, blizzard, tsunami, tornado, or earthquake. Any library can suffer from localized disasters such as a mold outbreak, flooding from water pipes, bug infestation, or computer hacking. Unfortunately, libraries must be cognizant of disasters caused by humankind as well, either of a terroristic nature or unintentional, such as a chemical spill or leak. Libraries, by their very nature, are a service industry, offering valuable resources to users. Preparing for disasters of any scale ensures that libraries can continue to offer their services, even when they are challenged.

Risk Assessment and Continuity of Operations Plans

The 2005 Neal-Schuman book *Disaster Planning: A How-To-Do-It Manual for Librarians* focused on creating a reactionary plan for responding to a disaster of any size. In this book, planning is taken a step further, focusing on Continuity of Operations (COOP) plans. As defined by the U.S. federal government (http://www.fema.gov/about/org/ncp/coop/index.shtm), COOP is an effort within an agency or institution to ensure that primary missions continue to be performed during a wide range of emergencies, including localized acts of nature, accidents, and technological or attack-related emergencies. COOP encompasses specific elements of continuity capabilities, including these:

IN THIS CHAPTER:

✓ Steps in Risk Assessment
✓ Conclusion
✓ References

- Essential functions: a subset of critical activities that are determined to be necessary to maintain primary institutional operations
- Orders of succession: identification of who assumes authority and responsibility of the organization, especially if key staff become incapacitated
- Delegation of authority: establishment of who has the right to make key decisions during a continuity situation
- Continuity facilities: alternate facilities where the organization can perform essential functions
- Continuity communications: availability and redundancy of critical communication systems to internal and external organizations, clients, and the public
- Vital records management: identification, protection, and availability of vital documents in both electronic and paper formats
- Human capital: identification of key staff needed to maintain operations
- Training and exercises: proper training needed to ensure key staff know what to do in the event of a disaster

- Devolution of control and direction: ability to transfer authority to outside sources, if necessary
- Reconstruction: the process of bringing the institution back to normal operational status

In simple terms, COOP is the process by which a library can get back to business in the aftermath of a disaster. Risk assessment, the necessary first step in COOP, is addressed in this chapter. Additional chapters cover other steps in the process, such as responding to threats, obtaining assistance, and leveraging the library. By making an initial investment of time to develop a COOP plan, libraries can ensure that they will be ready to resume essential activities and perhaps even introduce new, needed services immediately following a crisis. While planning of any sort is often sacrificed in lieu of other daily activities, an important mantra to remember is that *it was not raining when Noah began building the ark.*

Active Shooter at the Texas Medical Center Library in Houston

On September 28, 2010, during a meeting of the Texas Council of State University Librarians at a hotel on the University of Texas campus in Austin, an armed gunman, reminiscent of the 2007 attack at Virginia Tech, stormed into the Perry-Castañeda Library after releasing shots on campus. With all campus buildings locked down, the gunman tragically took his own life on the sixth floor of the library; fortunately, no other lives were lost. Many of the librarians in lockdown at the hotel were heard discussing their library's lack of a policy on how to react in an active shooting situation. While the Texas Medical Center Library in Houston does have an active shooter policy, it had been filed away for about two years without anyone having thought about reviewing it or conducting a drill to see if it was viable. Immediately upon returning to Houston, plans were set in place to meet with local law enforcement officials to reexamine the policy.

This unfortunate incident proved that anything can happen at any time. In a survey of the council, it was revealed that many of respondents had a disaster plan, but only about half included a policy on active shooters. Several of the library directors responded that their disaster plan was part of an overall university system plan that included a policy for responding to an active shooter threat. Other directors responded that they had neither a disaster plan nor an active shooter policy. At first glance, an active shooter might not be considered to have the same impact on library services as a natural disaster. However, the suspension of library services for the duration of the event and the subsequent investigation, particularly in cases when the library is part of the crime scene, certainly affects the ability of the library staff to conduct business. This incident also serves as a valuable reminder that there are a number of crises that can affect a library, many that library management might never think about. Therefore, the first step in the disaster planning process is to assess the potential risks to the organization that could result in disasters or emergency situations. It is necessary to consider all of the possible incident types, as well as the impact each may have on the library's ability to continue to deliver its normal services.

—Deborah Halsted
Senior Associate Director, Operations
The Texas Medical Center Library
Houston, TX

The primary responsibility for all planning, including risk assessment, resides with the library director, management staff, and governing body. Even when the library's disaster plan is included in the larger entity's (city, county, university, hospital, school district, law firm, etc.) overall plan, the unique features of a library require that specialized plans are also in place to deal with collections and continuity of service. Recent experiences illustrate that following a disaster of any size dependence on a library's facility and resources often increases, as was seen by libraries around the country following Hurricane Katrina. Increased demand is likely to be seen not only for traditional library services but also for new service roles as well. Examples include:

- Computers and Internet access to facilitate:

  - communication with family members, friends, and colleagues
  - identification of resources, such as insurance, shelters, and assistance from the American Red Cross, Federal Emergency Management Agency (FEMA), and other agencies
  - location of necessary forms, which could be printed or filled out online

- Electricity to recharge cell phones, laptops, tablets, and other devices
- Shelter from the elements, including heat, rain, and wind
- Access to print and/or electronic resources for a variety of users, including:

  - first responders dealing with illness, injuries, and so forth in the affected population
  - individuals affected by the disaster who may have an acute need for recreational reading

- Diversionary programs such as storytimes for displaced children and families
- Day-care services for first responders and other workers/volunteers contributing to recovery and response efforts
- Location of the emergency operations center for the response team

The Library's Role in Crisis

"Public libraries are a natural haven for the community. During times of crisis, though, the role of the library is essential not only in providing a wide range of needed resources and services; it is also about offering a place of calm, togetherness, and sense of community."

("Narratives from the Storm," 2008)

COOP should always include a risk assessment of all possible threats and consideration of the potential damage or interruption of services and available mitigation options. Risk assessment is a process in which library staff, facility experts, and outside authorities determine potential events that could cause service interruption. These events can include natural disasters such as an earthquake, hurricane, or flood; bug or mold infestation; fire and the results of extinguishing the fire; acts of terrorism; and threats to the information technology infrastructure (table 1.1).

Risk assessment is a prevalent activity in many fields. For example, the U.S. National Library of Medicine offers risk assessment and regulation information in various resources in its TOXNET family of databases (http://sis.nlm.nih.gov/enviro/riskinformation.html). The U.S. Environmental Protection Agency offers basic information about environmental

TABLE 1.1 Possible Events Causing Service Interruption

Environmental	Human	Loss of Utilities or Services	Equipment Failure	Other
Blizzard	Active shooter	Electricity	Cybercrime	Health epidemic
Earthquake	Arson	Fuel	HVAC system	Public transportation disruption
Flood	Labor dispute	Internet service	Internal electrical infrastructure	Toxic releases
Hurricane	Terrorism	Natural gas	IT network	
Landslide	Theft	Telephone service	Loss of records or data	
Mold	War	Water		
Pest infestation	Workplace violence			
Tornado				
Tsunami				
Wildfire				

risk assessments for the public, along with tools, guidance, and guidelines (http://www.epa.gov/risk/). The U.S. Food and Drug Administration regulates food and drug safety through risk assessment (http://www.fda.gov/food/foodscienceresearch/risksafetyassessment/default.htm). Risk assessment is also incorporated into project management, information security, and even in something as simple as planning a wedding.

Regardless of the exact context, any risk assessment project should include a study of the likelihood of the risk occurring and the impact if it does. Greatest efforts should be targeted to those events with the highest probability and impact (Breighner and Payton, 2005).

The risk assessment process should also include mitigation, or ways to avoid certain risks and ways to lessen the impact in the event of a disaster. Mitigation is often a required step when requesting funding from a federal agency such as FEMA to aid recovery efforts following a major disaster. For example, if in the assessment process it is determined that the library is subject to flooding, flood walls can be constructed around the facility to lessen the threat.

When beginning a risk assessment process there are eight recommended steps. These steps, which are discussed in the following section, provide an introduction to what needs to be in place prior to proceeding with COOP. These steps can also be used when conducting a risk assessment for any facility, including your home. While some steps might need to be adjusted, such as creating the risk assessment planning team, the concepts are valid regardless of the setting being assessed.

Steps in Risk Assessment

These are the eight essential steps in conducting a risk assessment:

1. Create a risk assessment planning team
2. Identify possible hazards
3. Conduct a vulnerability analysis
4. Analyze current strengths and weaknesses
5. Inventory assets and estimate possible losses
6. Conduct an insurance assessment
7. Consider mitigation options (including Incident Command System training)
8. Review and update

Step 1: Create a Risk Assessment Planning Team

Establishing a risk assessment team prior to the actual disaster planning process allows libraries to identify the possible situations that might affect an individual library and then build or modify that library's plan based on the likely risks. While the risk assessment team will contain many of the same people who are on the disaster planning team, the makeup of each group may vary depending on the size of the library and on the level of involvement of the parent institution.

Key members for the risk assessment team are described next, keeping in mind that adjustments should be made as needed based on the size of the library. For instance, in a smaller library, one person may serve in multiple roles. In the case of a one-person library, help might be needed from outside the library, drawing on expertise from the parent organization, city, county, and so forth.

Library director: The library director is ultimately responsible for the library and all contents and should ensure that a risk assessment takes place. Depending on the type of library, though, other entities, such as a university, city or county government, or corporation, might assume the overall responsibility for disaster planning and risk assessment. Even so, it is the responsibility of the director to certify that the library is involved in the planning and implementation of a disaster response. The director also leads all efforts in the library, including appointing the risk assessment team, following up on recommendations, and filtering the information gathered by the team for higher authorities.

Property manager/head of facilities: The property manager should be the person most familiar with the library building, the heating, ventilation, and air conditioning (HVAC) system, the electrical system, the grounds, and so forth. This person is in the best position to assess the effects of incidents on the facility and its contents. The property manager, in consultation with public officials or higher authorities, is the most likely person to close the library in the event of an impending disaster or after an event.

Safety manager: Safety is the most important element of any event. An institutional safety manager, or an outside consultant, is vital in evaluating the library and assisting in making it safer should disaster strike. A safety manager can help assess mitigation efforts, such as a sprinkler system, and identify potential hazards, like unsecured outside furniture, garbage receptacles, or inadequate emergency exits.

Comptroller/accountant: The comptroller is responsible for all financial aspects of the library and may not be a member of the library staff. In larger entities, this individual is often part of a division that serves the entire organization. Regardless, the comptroller is responsible for maintaining an up-to-date inventory, with value added, of all the library's possessions, including print collections, special collections, equipment, furniture, and the library structure itself. The comptroller is also responsible for communicating with insurance agencies, whether the institution is self-insured or insured by a private company. Part of the risk assessment process is to confirm that the library has adequate insurance to cover any and all losses.

Information technology director: The information technology (IT) director is an essential member of the risk management team because libraries and library clients have become so dependent on electronic resources to accomplish daily activities. One of the primary responsibilities for the IT director is to establish an infrastructure for offering access to resources and services in the event of a disaster. For many libraries a priority component of the organization's technology infrastructure is the colocation of essential resources either at a facility on a separate electrical grid from the library or in a virtual form utilizing cloud computing. In addition, the IT director should design an infrastructure with the flexibility to accommodate key staff members who need to work remotely if the library is not accessible.

Hurricane Ike in Houston and Galveston

In 2008, Hurricane Ike created a massive power outage in the greater Houston-Galveston, Texas, area, which made many essential web-based services unavailable. Thanks to lessons learned from previous tropical events, both the Moody Medical Library of the University of Texas Medical Branch in Galveston and the Texas Medical Center Library in Houston had colocated access for electronic resources to facilities outside the geographic area. In the case of the Texas Medical Center Library, a greatly scaled down website was available to anyone with electricity and an Internet connection. Most of the institutions at the Texas Medical Center mitigated loss of utilities by burying all electrical cables belowground after Tropical Storm Allison in 2001. This advance planning provided the required infrastructure health-care professionals needed in order to access the library's vital electronic resources.

−J. Chris Young
Associate Director, Information Technology and Institutional Relations
The Texas Medical Center Library
Houston, TX

Human resources representative: Without question a library's staff is the most important resource. For this reason, the human resources (HR) representative should be on the risk assessment team to help identify the employees who are essential to maintaining resources and services following an event. The HR representative must also plan for backup staff in case key people are unable to report to work due to personal damage, loss, or evacuation. The HR representative may also coordinate consultations with local and regional authorities about the types of disasters that could affect the library (see table 1.2). The HR representative may invite authorities such as local emergency managers, climatologists, first responders, and fire and police department officials to meetings or encourage the risk management team to open other communication channels or utilize resources online to assist with planning efforts.

A final element of developing the risk assessment team is to establish who has the highest authority, which should be the library director or the property manager. In many cases these two positions will share joint authority, with the library director being in charge of the library contents and the property manager responsible for the facility.

TABLE 1.2   Outside Experts

Expert	Role
Community emergency management office	The community emergency management office is the best place to determine possible threats. Much of this information can be found on its website, but, if possible, try to meet with a representative. There are two reasons for this. First, you will get more information in a one-on-one meeting. Second, a meeting will allow you to describe possible services the library can offer before, during, and after a disaster. Often, the library is forgotten in large-scale emergency planning.
Mayor or community administrator	A meeting with the mayor may be unlikely, particularly in larger communities, but the mayor's office will be a source of resources and services in the event of a regional disaster. Consult the mayor's website or call the office for more information.
Community Emergency Response Team (CERT)	Most communities now have CERTs that are composed of volunteers who are committed to assisting the community in the event of a disaster. Many librarians are now volunteering for local CERTs, allowing them to become integrated into local efforts before a disaster occurs.
Fire department	The fire department can offer facility assessment and valuable training, such as what to do in a fire, evacuation procedures, and safe usage of fire extinguishers.
Police department	A representative from the police department or campus security can help plan a response to local threats, such as an active shooter or any dangerous or disruptive client.
Public works department	Public works personnel can help with identification of local utilities, such as water and sewer, that are essential for library operations.
Emergency medical services	Know the location of the nearest emergency medical services personnel likely to respond to any personal injury in the library.
American Red Cross	The American Red Cross excels in disaster response and has many resources available to assist with COOP and risk assessment.
FEMA	While you probably will not meet with FEMA prior to an event, its website has valuable resources, including *Emergency Management Guide for Business and Industry: A Step-by-Step Approach to Emergency, Planning, Response and Recovery for Companies of All Sizes* (http://www.fema.gov/pdf/library/bizindst.pdf).

(Continued)

TABLE 1.2 Outside Experts *(Continued)*

Expert	Role
National Weather Service	The National Weather Service, along with local media, should be your primary resource for monitoring local weather events.
Planning commission	The local planning commission will have information on mitigation efforts like improved drainage and sewer lines and stabilization of electrical utilities.
Telephone company	Keep a portable record of telephone company contacts so that you can reach someone remotely, even if you cannot enter the library. You can work to restore connectivity even before being allowed back in. See chapter 4.
Utilities	As with the telephone company, similar procedures should be followed.
Neighboring institutions	Get to know your institutional neighbors! They can be vital resources before, during, and after an event. (For example, following Tropical Storm Allison, the Texas Medical Center Library was the only building in the immediate vicinity with running water, making the public restrooms very popular with neighboring institutions.)

Step 2: Identify Possible Hazards

A good place to begin assembling information on possible hazards and emergencies is to brainstorm with current staff and consult with local experts. Potential hazards to consider include those caused by environmental factors, those caused by humans, and situations created by loss of utilities or equipment. Other scenarios, such as a pandemic flu outbreak, should also be analyzed because they could greatly reduce your workforce or close your facility completely.

Past history and geography will make planning for some hazards obvious, such as hurricanes on the Gulf of Mexico or tornadoes in Oklahoma, but planners must also think outside the box. For example, recent violent tornadoes in Massachusetts surprised even the most seasoned disaster planners. Meeting with local experts can ensure that libraries do not overlook or minimize potential risks. No library wants to experience an active shooter, but meeting with police will help risk assessment team members plan a response in the event that it happens. Libraries are very public places and are susceptible to anyone entering the facility who wishes to inflict harm. Additionally, while not every library is vulnerable to flooding due to external sources, a meeting with the facilities manager can update the risk assessment team on the age of internal plumbing and the possibility of a major water leak. Fire is always a possibility, so meeting with the local fire department can help identify and mitigate risks and assess if the current fire suppression system is adequate or if it would cause more destruction than necessary if activated.

Checklist for Identifying Disaster Restoration Partners

Before a disaster strikes it is very important to identify disaster restoration companies that will help you with the recovery process. Here are some things to keep in mind when meeting with contractors.

- ❑ Is the library on more than one disaster restoration company's priority list? During a community-wide disaster, resources get tapped out very quickly.
- ❑ Do key team members understand the library's insurance policy?
- ❑ Does the library have a special paper or a document recovery/book recovery policy? Document restoration is very expensive.
- ❑ Are key team members familiar with current pricing for disaster recovery resources and services? This knowledge is the best protection against price gouging.
- ❑ Know the capabilities of the disaster restoration company or companies that may be employed. Obtain references up front on their completed projects in similar facilities. Ask lots of questions!
- ❑ What type of insurance does the company carry? It is standard practice for a company to provide proof of insurance before a job begins.
- ❑ What part of the project, if any, will be subcontracted out? Make sure any subcontractors meet the library's standards.
- ❑ Establish both client and contractor expectations before work begins.

By considering these points before disaster restoration services are needed library staff can make rational, informed decisions and ensure that the recovery process proceeds faster and more efficiently.

−Kari Menster
Priority Response Coordinator
Blackmon Mooring of Houston
Houston, TX

Step 3: Conduct a Vulnerability Analysis

The next step in risk assessment is to evaluate the library's vulnerability, including the probability and potential impact of each type of emergency. Recognizing the most vulnerable areas will better equip staff members to plan for and protect against possible damage and destruction.

Table 1.3 offers a guide to the process of recording a library's unique vulnerabilities, estimating the impacts, and assessing resources using a numerical system. The lower the score the better, with 1 representing the lowest impact in each category and 5 the highest.

TABLE 1.3 Vulnerability Table for Houston, Texas

Type of Emergency	Probability	Human Impact	Property Impact	Service Impact	Internal Resources	External Resources	Total
	High = 5 Low = 1	High = 5 Low = 1	High = 5 Low = 1	High = 5 Low = 1	Weak = 5 Strong = 1	Weak = 5 Strong = 1	
Hurricane	5	5	5	5	2	2	24
Blizzard	1	3	2	2	2	3	13
Terrorism	4	5	5	5	2	1	22
Mold	3	3	3	2	2	2	15
Earthquake	1	1	1	1	1	1	6
Power outage	3	5	3	5	3	3	19

The first column of the chart includes a list of probable emergencies that could affect a specific facility, including those which could occur inside the facility as well as those caused by external factors. Consider historical events such as wildfires, hurricanes, blizzards, toxic releases, terrorism, and recurrent power outages. Also think about the potential for elevated risk based on geographic proximity to a fault line; companies that produce, store, or transport hazardous materials; major transportation facilities; high-profile facilities; or nuclear power plants. Other potential hazards to keep in mind are technological failures due to fire or explosion; failure of telecommunication, power, or HVAC systems; and IT infrastructure crashes due to hardware failure, computer viruses, or other malware. Based on the input of local experts and the risk assessment team, the vulnerability analysis chart should list all potential events for your geographic area.

In the second column of the chart, rank the probability of each individual emergency. Input from local officials and the property manager can provide assistance in completing this section.

In the next three columns, record estimates for the human, property, and service impacts of each type of emergency. The human impact includes the possibility of injury or death. The property impact includes the cost to repair, replace, or set up a temporary replacement. Both human and property estimates have an effect on the potential loss of business. Areas to consider when estimating service impact include business interruption, employees unable to report for work, and interruption of services offered to clients.

In the next two columns, consider internal and external resources to address the emergency and rank their availability, with 5 being the weakest and 1 being the strongest. Resources may include staff expertise, colocated electronic resources, an existing contract with a disaster recovery firm, or a current COOP plan.

Finally, to assess the vulnerability for each possible event, simply add the figures in each row and record the total in the final column. The potential disasters with the highest scores, usually over 20, should be emphasized in COOP. Those with low scores, under 10, may be addressed but will not be the primary focus in terms of risk assessment.

Step 4: Analyze Current Strengths and Weaknesses

COOP requires the analysis of current capabilities and hazards. This process consists of gathering information about existing strengths, weaknesses, and possible emergencies and then conducting a vulnerability analysis to determine your capability for handling and mitigating emergencies. This step also includes identifying current staff member strengths, such as a medical or nursing background and communications or foreign language skills.

Begin this process by reviewing internal plans and policies, such as the evacuation plan, sprinkler system layout and operation, security procedures, video surveillance system, insurance policies, finance and purchasing procedures, and current emergency contact lists for staff and vendors. The Pocket Response Plan (PReP) (http://www.statearchivists.org/prepare/framework/prep.htm), created by the Council of State Archivists (CoSA), is a concise document for recording essential information needed by staff in case of a disaster. The PReP is customizable for each institution and is discussed in more detail in chapter 4.

Additionally, many disaster recovery firms offer special programs for preferred customers. Two examples, Code Blue from Polygon (http://www.polygongroup.com/us/our-services/code-blue/) and BELFOR's Red Alert (http://www.belfor.com/Uploads/Documents/RedAlert.pdf), offer preferential service to customers who sign a contract in advance. In the case of these two companies, there is no annual fee to be on the preferred customer list.

Next, identify critical library services and operations. This information is necessary to assess the impact of potential emergencies and to determine the need for backup operations. These services include:

- What is needed to continue to offer resources and services, such as reference services, access to electronic collections, document delivery, and interlibrary loan, if the library is *closed*
- Products and services offered by major vendors, especially sole-source vendors
- Lifeline services such as electricity, water, sewer, gas, and telecommunications
- Personnel and equipment needed to maintain basic services

Once you have identified vital services, you must identify internal and external resources and capabilities already in place to support these services, including:

- Personnel: IT staff to maintain critical systems and infrastructure, reference staff to provide instruction or mediated searches, security staff to maintain a safe facility, an evacuation team, public information officer, and so forth
- Equipment and supplies: fire detection and sprinkler system, communications equipment such as a public address system and text-enabled cell phones, proxy server, and first aid kit
- Facilities: emergency operations center (see discussion of NIMS ICS in chapter 7), media briefing area (if appropriate), shelter areas, first aid stations, and sanitary facilities
- Organizational capabilities: training, drills, evacuation plan, Employee Assistance Program
- Backup systems: payroll, communications, customer service, shipping and receiving, IT support, emergency power, and recovery services
- Local agencies such as emergency management, fire, police, community service organizations, contractors, and disaster response companies
- National organizations such as the American Red Cross and FEMA

Step 5: Inventory Assets and Estimate Possible Losses

To mitigate or recover from a disaster, first assess what is owned. Every library should have a current inventory of all assets, including the facility, print and electronic collections, special collections, equipment, furniture, and supplies. The inventory should include a valuation of worth and be presented to the institutional insurance carrier, whether self-insured or insured by an insurance company. In this assessment, identify the most critical possessions and create a salvage plan with details about how to save priority items should disaster strike. Priority items may include the proxy server, irreplaceable rare collections, payroll and tax records, and contracts with essential vendors along with contact information for key agents. Completion of a thorough inventory is critical before proceeding to the next step, insurance assessment.

Step 6: Conduct an Insurance Assessment

The insurance assessment process for the library is the same process that individuals should conduct for homes and personal items. Even if the facility is not owned by the library, regular assessment of the real property that is owned by the library must be conducted to ensure adequate insurance coverage.

There are two types of property, real and personal. Real property, owned or leased, comprises the building, buildings under construction, office facilities, storage facilities, and garages. It also includes permanently affixed equipment, fire detection and suppression systems, HVAC systems, and external fixtures such as antennae or flag poles. Personal property includes anything that is portable or not permanently affixed, such as furniture, books, special collections, fine art, shelving, computers, business records, supplies, exhibits, and motor vehicles, such as a library van or a bookmobile. The risk assessment team should work with the insurance carrier on an annual basis to confirm that all real and personal property are insured at a level that allows for replacement at current market value.

Step 7: Consider Mitigation Options

Once assessments of probable risks are conducted, it is a good idea to examine possible methods for mitigating future damage to the structure and contents and for lessening the chance of personal injury. Some solutions are easy and relatively cheap, such as securing any outside furniture in patios or courtyards so they do not move or become airborne in high winds. More extensive, and expensive, mitigation efforts include installing flood walls and gates in an area prone to flooding or installing a dry-pipe fire suppression system. For example, after extensive regional power outages in the greater Houston area following Tropical Storm Allison in 2001, the Texas Medical Center spent many years and much money moving electrical facilities to the upper floors of all buildings and burying electrical lines belowground to protect them from falling limbs and trees. As a result, the medical center never lost power during Hurricane Ike in 2008, which allowed the vital medical infrastructure to remain intact when most other entities were out of business.

While mitigation can be expensive, there are agencies such as FEMA that can help. Before applying, planners must be aware of specific regulations for receiving funding from these agencies. For example, to qualify for funding from FEMA, an institution must be National Incident Management System (NIMS) Incident Command System (ICS) compliant and use the appropriate ICS forms. The NIMS ICS structure is discussed in chapter 7.

Step 8: Review and Update

A risk assessment, like a disaster plan, must be updated on a regular basis. It is obvious that the inventory will change from year to year, so it is suggested that an inventory be conducted at the beginning of each fiscal year. On the other hand, equipment will devalue each year, especially computer equipment. An insurance adjustment should be completed annually depending on aging equipment or replacement of old equipment. Contact information changes more rapidly than anything else and should be updated at least quarterly.

Conclusion

Conducting a risk assessment of a facility, determining the abilities of staff members, and implementing mitigation efforts will help minimize damage or destruction from a disaster. This risk assessment should not be done in a vacuum but by an internal team with the input of local and regional experts. If the facility is part of a larger system, the team will also include input from close institutional colleagues. The risk assessment, like the disaster or COOP plan, must be updated regularly to ensure its validity.

Following the risk assessment process, library managers should next determine core services offered to clients. These core services can take place in house or be incorporated into remote services that can address needs if the actual facility is closed for any period of time. In times of crisis, core services may need to be enhanced or modified to fill gaps or provide new options for people displaced by the event. The provision of both core and unique services is the focus of chapter 2.

References

Breighner, Mary, and William Payton. 2005. *Risk and Insurance Management Manual for Libraries*. Chicago: American Library Association.

"Narratives from the Storm." 2008. *Texas Library Journal* 84, no. 4: 162–165.

Responding to a Threat

Your mettle will be judged on your ability to respond to an incident with little or no warning.

—Daniel T. Wilson

Most writings on disaster planning cover the four elements of the emergency management cycle: preparedness, response, recovery, and mitigation, as shown in figure 2.1.

IN THIS CHAPTER:

- ✓ The Importance of Immediate Responses
- ✓ Planning Responses Based on Potential Risks
- ✓ Designing Drills to Assist in Training for Response
- ✓ After-Action Review
- ✓ Conclusion
- ✓ References

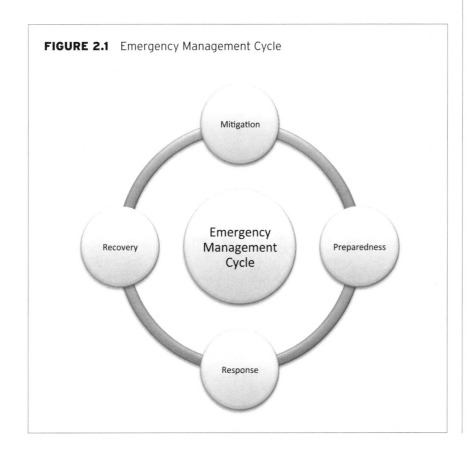

FIGURE 2.1 Emergency Management Cycle

The emphasis of this book is on the preparedness and response elements of the emergency management cycle. The book addresses mitigation activities when discussing the preparedness and response aspects but leaves coverage of recovery planning to other works on the subject. This chapter identifies different types of threats and then groups them by the type of anticipated warning in order to assist in writing and executing a specific plan. Included are sample drills and tabletop exercises (TTEs) and information about the importance of an after-action review (AAR). At the end of the chapter is a very useful tool, a response table that can be adapted to your environment. A commitment to creating a response table for your institution should be a high-priority item in the emergency planning process.

The Importance of Immediate Responses

How you and your staff react to a threat is paramount to the success of your response plan. Inability to react appropriately may lead to damage to the facility or collections and could contribute to injury or death. It is important to keep in mind that staff members have limited control over the circumstances of an emergency situation. Staff responsible for conducting an evacuation of a facility, for example, should be made aware that they are not personally responsible for ensuring that all members of the public have left the building. Their role is to inform the occupants of the building and to facilitate the evacuation by giving directions, assisting where needed, and then ensuring their own personal safety by exiting the building. Occupants who do not leave the building when requested are assuming responsibility for their own safety and will likely be chastised by first responders when they arrive on the scene. Check with local law enforcement officials to confirm that this strategy reflects the appropriate plan of action for your institution.

One of the most challenging aspects of planning for emergency response is ensuring that whenever your library is open it is staffed at all times by someone who has been trained to respond to threats. The title of this person's role can vary, but common designations include emergency response coordinator or building marshal. Multiple staff members need to be identified as emergency response coordinators in order to provide coverage for this important role during all hours for which the library is open. When the library is fully staffed the role may be filled by a senior administrator, but during weekend or evening hours the role may be filled by the library's desk staff or a student assistant. The essential quality required of all individuals assigned to this role is that they are trained to respond effectively to emergencies.

How someone naturally reacts to an emergency situation is very important since everyone will not respond in a calm and thoughtful way. Therefore, it is important to understand the strengths and weaknesses of staff assigned to coordinate a response. Marty Thompson, retired Director of the Robert M. Bird Library at the University of Oklahoma Health Sciences

Center and a frequent speaker about emergency preparedness and response, draws on his military experience when he notes that not everyone is "wired" to lead troops into battle. It is important to train those who are capable of taking on this responsibility and to be sure that those who will not be the leaders at least know what needs to be done. Realistically, considering staffing constraints in many libraries, it may not be possible to have someone with leadership skills always available to handle emergency response. The best advice is to maximize the capabilities of all staff members and prepare everyone to contribute to planning and response efforts in some way.

A case study for the importance of being prepared for an appropriate emergency response is illustrated by an event that occurred in March 2009 at the Cologne Archives in Cologne, Germany. The Cologne Archives building was constructed in1971 to hold myriad archival materials, some of which dated back to 922 AD. The building was located in downtown Cologne next to a tunnel that was being excavated for a subway line. On the afternoon of March 3, construction workers noticed large cracks appearing in the building structure and they notified Archives staff and patrons of the impending disaster. Three minutes later, the building collapsed. Two people died, both of whom were in an attached adjacent building; however, all Archives staff and visitors were able to escape the six-story building.

Three minutes may not sound like a lot of time, but, in fact, a lot can happen in three minutes. Think of your library. Could you evacuate all patrons and staff within three minutes on a busy weekday afternoon? It may be helpful to use this three-minute measure to guide your evacuation planning efforts.

On March 1, 2008, in Americus, Georgia, a tornado destroyed Sumter Regional Hospital. The EF3 tornado was approximately one-mile wide and was on the ground for nearly 40 miles. Although two people lost their lives near the hospital, there were no fatalities in the hospital because of the way the nurses reacted to the tornado warning, directing all patients and visitors to move away from windows. Examples such as these prompt questions about whether libraries have procedures in place to respond appropriately and quickly to a tornado warning. If there was a tornado warning in effect for your library, would employees be prepared to help patrons take shelter in a safe place?

Planning Responses Based on Potential Risks

The examples described depict successful reactions to an imminent threat. Fortunately, not all risks require a reactionary response. Some potential risks provide ample lead time for careful planning and mitigation, whereas others offer no warning. When faced with a sudden emergency, those responding may be at the mercy of the situation, but even for unforeseen events, carrying out plans that have been put in place ahead of time can help to mitigate the impact and improve outcomes.

Continued on p. 21

Categorizing Potential Risks

Following is a list of potential risks that were introduced in the previous chapter and can be considered either a disaster or a major cause of service disruption. Notice how these risks can be grouped into three categories: advance warning, little warning, and no warning, with some risks falling into more than one category. Grouping risks this way will help with emergency planning, since response procedures will be similar within each group.

Advance warning:
- Severe weather
- Flood
- Riots and mobs
- Hurricane
- Wildfire
- Furlough days
- System upgrades
- Labor dispute
- Epidemic/pandemic

Little advance warning:
- Tsunami
- Active shooter
- Tornado
- Riots and mobs
- Bomb threat

No warning:
- Earthquake
- Landslide
- Arson
- Active shooter
- Bioterrorism
- Cyberterrorism
- Bombing
- Riots and mobs
- Workplace violence
- Hostage situation
- HVAC failure
- Loss of power
- IT network outage
- HAZMAT incident
- Water main break
- Sewer backup
- Public transportation incident/disruption

Planning for Events with Advance Warning

Some events provide advance warning, which affords the opportunity to plan ahead. Of these events, one of the most common and destructive is a hurricane. Fortunately, modern storm tracking technologies make it possible to ascertain areas of risk in order to facilitate planning. Other types of disasters that offer advance warning include severe winter storms and pandemics.

Weather-Related Events

Hurricanes can be quite destructive. Indeed, in a post on Forbes.com on September 13, 2008, titled "America's Most Expensive Natural Disasters," Matt Woolsey notes that hurricanes rank as the deadliest and costliest disasters (Woolsey, 2008). However, in most cases, there will be several days to prepare for hurricanes, as their paths are somewhat predictable. Hurricanes, like the other risks in the advance warning category, usually require no reactionary response procedures because of the availability of weather reports. Even these relatively slow-moving storms do, however, require carefully thought-out response procedures as well as mitigation steps.

Public Health Events

In the summer of 2009, many libraries worldwide were preparing to deal with possible consequences of the H1N1 influenza ("swine flu") pandemic. An example of the types of plans that were being made can be found on a website produced by the Wisconsin Department of Public Instruction, which released guidelines for public libraries specifically urging libraries to work with their municipalities "to determine what services the library might be expected to provide in the event of a pandemic outbreak in the community" (Wisconsin Department of Public Instruction, 2014). In addition, the American Library Association (2011) advised its members to develop policies to address the following issues:

- Criteria for closing the library
- Employee policies for sick leave, payroll and banking/financial issues, and working from home
- Mandated documentation of procedures or cross-training so others can take over for sick employees
- Policies for "social distancing" to keep people and their belongings separate from one another, such as removing a number of chairs so people are not sitting close to each other, limiting the number of people who can come in at any one time, or taking out coat racks
- Criteria for suspending storytimes and other library programs
- Providing masks and gloves and training staff in the removal and disposal of these items
- Standards for cleaning bathrooms, railings and door knobs, telephones, keyboards, counters, and the work areas of employees who go home sick, including emptying wastebaskets
- Setting a schedule for addressing critical facility and administrative needs if the library is closed for an extended period (boiler and building checks by custodians, book drop, payroll and banking considerations)
- Communications plan for reaching staff and informing the public
- Means for continuing to provide information services for the public, such as online ordering of materials and alternate pick-up/drop-off locations for materials or expansion of online services
- Accommodation of the needs of disadvantaged people in the community who may not have personal access to materials such as the local newspaper or resources like a home computer
- Education of the public in advance of a widespread public health event

Continued from p. 20

collection for storage in the event of a hurricane. To prepare for Hurricane Dolly, this select group of print resources was placed in a secure location on the second floor of the building along with laptop computers and other critical equipment. In the event that the facility sustained significant damage, these resources would be used to establish a small functioning library in an alternate location.

The remaining collection was covered and secured with plastic sheeting and tarps. Materials located on bottom shelves were moved to the shelves above and covered. All desktop computers and electronics were unplugged, moved away from windows and doorways, and covered with plastic sheeting for protection. (Wilson, 2008)

The storm closed the library, not because of wind, but because of major water damage. With the small collection of books and laptops that had been secured before the storm, library staff members were able to continue to provide services from an alternate location. Thirty days after the storm, a portion of the library reopened and normal services were restored. However, because of ongoing repairs, the entire library did not open for another three months.

Other library organizations were also involved in pandemic preparedness planning. The National Emergency Preparedness and Response Initiative for the National Network of Libraries of Medicine created a pandemic preparedness table (table 2.1) based on the pandemic stages table released by the World Health Organization (WHO).

On August 10, 2010, WHO Director-General Margaret Chan announced that the H1N1 virus had moved into the post-pandemic period; however, she cautioned, localized incidents are likely to happen. "As we enter the post-pandemic period, this does not mean that the H1N1 virus has gone away. Based on experience with past pandemics, we expect the H1N1 virus to take on the behaviour of a seasonal influenza virus and continue to circulate for some years to come" (World Health Organization, 2010).

Other illnesses that could require a public health emergency response would be an *E. coli* outbreak, food chain terrorism, and superbugs, which are bacteria that are resistant to antibiotics. Each of these risks has the

TABLE 2.1 Pandemic Planning: Stages of Pandemic and Library Procedures

Period	Level	Description	Procedures
Prepandemic	1	New influenza virus is detected, no vaccination is available, and it begins to spread among humans in a limited area.	Monitor information sources about the situation (CDC, institution), with no changes to operations.
Pandemic alert	2	The virus poses a substantial risk of transmission and spreads rapidly beyond the locality of origin. The public is informed that a new virus is successfully spreading.	Continue to monitor information sources, no changes to operations.
	3	The virus spreads globally, is transmitted quickly among humans, and creates widespread infection.	Develop/review pandemic plans and schedule a tabletop exercise involving relevant personnel for dealing with the potential effects of the new virus (staff absences, limited hours of operation, closure due to social distancing measures). Update procedures as necessary. If feasible, enable connectivity for designated staff to online library resources from their homes. Create a prioritized list of supplies and order additional essential supplies, anticipating possible interruptions of service from vendors.

TABLE 2.1 Pandemic Planning: Stages of Pandemic and Library Procedures *(Continued)*

Period	Level	Description	Procedures
Pandemic	4	The WHO declares the virus to be a global pandemic.	Managers meet to discuss strategies for: 1. slowing the spread of the virus, and 2. dealing with a significant rate of staff absences. Based on existing variables, managers decide whether, when, and how changes to operations will be made as the situation evolves. Measures intended to slow the spread of the virus may include reduction of hours of operation, closure of service desks, and removal of shared equipment in public areas. Anticipating staffing shortages, managers ascertain institutional and organizational personnel and staffing policies and procedures in order to continue to offer limited library services (e.g., time and leave requirements for faculty and staff to work from home, designating essential personnel, circumstances for which leave requests may or may not be approved). Establish a deep chain-of-command so that if key library managers are ill and unable to perform their duties a structure for decision making and communication can be maintained. Order any essential supplies that may be needed to fill possible shortfalls from vendors.
	5	Virus becomes prevalent in the local community and authorities invoke measures in order to slow the spread of the virus. Operations may be affected by a significant rate of staff absenteeism.	Library managers comply with all directives from the institution about changes to operations resulting from the pandemic, adjusting operations and staffing patterns as the situation evolves. Measures to prevent spread of the virus may be enacted (see Level 4). Based on available staff, managers make decisions about who will work from home and during what hours in order to provide limited patron services from off-site. Notify patrons of changes to library hours and availability of limited services from off-site. Edit the library's webpage to show the status of operations and the services and resources available.

Source: http://nnlm.gov/ep/pandemic-planning/.

potential to be dangerous and could be included in the "little advance warning" category.

When planning for any type of incident for which you would have advance notice, it is important to expect the worst and then be thankful if the worst does not happen. Being well prepared for the worst possible scenario can mean the difference between a catastrophic event and a minor emergency.

Planning for Events with Little Advance Warning

Your library's ability to respond to emergencies is measured by how well situations with little advance warning are handled. Types of incidents that occur with little warning can include tornadoes, tsunamis, an active shooter, strife and conflict, and bomb threats. Open communication is essential when responding to these incidents, specifically, communication between public safety agencies and the library. Fortunately, public warning systems have improved considerably. Many years ago, tornado warnings were provided by a system of people designated as "spotters," who were trained to watch the sky from the southwest whenever the National Weather Service (NWS) detected the potential for tornadic activity on radar. If a tornado was spotted, the local Weather Bureau (predecessor of the NWS) was notified, resulting in a warning to the general public. Today, sophisticated equipment, including Doppler radar, is used to detect tornadic activity. Tornado watches and warnings are now broadcast through a variety of media channels and alert systems.

Tornadoes

Tornadoes can be catastrophic, and while forecasters now announce warnings when conditions exist for the formation of a tornado, the paths and intensity levels of tornadoes can still be very unpredictable. Librarians should check with public safety personnel at their parent institutions or in their communities to determine what alerting systems exist for tornadoes in their areas and how these can be incorporated into planning.

University of Virginia Claude Moore Health Sciences Library Response to Tornado Warning

The designated Emergency Response Coordinator (ERC) should monitor weather-reporting stations for announcements of tornado watches and warnings during any time of unsettled or stormy weather. This occurs most often in spring and summer in our region but can happen at any time of year.

Our National Oceanic Atmospheric Administration (NOAA) All Hazards radio is in the bindery prep area behind the Library Service Desk (the only place where it receives a reliable signal). Whenever its alarm goes off, the ERC should be notified.

If a tornado warning is issued for the city of Charlottesville, the ERC should make the following announcement on the public address (PA) system:

Your attention please. A tornado warning has been posted for our immediate area. Please move away from windows and exterior doors at this time. Do not use elevators.

If a tornado is sighted or reported in the vicinity of the Library, the ERC should immediately announce tornado shelter-in-place procedures over the PA, or, if power is off, staff should use the bullhorn to inform patrons and staff, directing them to the appropriate shelter-in-place location.

—Susan Yowell
Circulation Manager
University of Virginia Claude Moore Health Sciences Library
Charlottesville, VA

Riots and Mobs

On Wednesday, June 15, 2011, riots broke out in Vancouver, Canada, following their hockey team's game seven loss in the Stanley Cup finals. Vehicles were overturned and burned, stores were looted, and police were confronted. Vancouver officials took steps to mediate the violence, such as limiting access to the area, but mayhem still ensued and several people were arrested and injured throughout the evening. Fortunately, the Vancouver Central Library suffered minimal damage during the riots, with only a short-term closure of the Children's Library because two windows were smashed.

On Thursday, December 10, 2009, over 600 students at Old Dominion University in Norfolk, Virginia, used social media to stage a flash mob at the Perry Library. Captured on video available through YouTube, the event resulted in a packed lobby and included crowd surfing. Police efforts to disperse the crowd failed, and they resorted to using pepper spray.

In some cases, flash mobs and riots can be anticipated, such as the Vancouver riots, or officials can catch wind of a flash mob through social media. Therefore, libraries have some advance notice and can prepare a strategy in order to minimize the impact of the event. Once again, talk to local law enforcement officials about appropriate procedures to put in place at your library. This is necessary because the physical structures of libraries differ, as do the environments surrounding them.

Perhaps the most difficult situation to plan for is an active shooter. The unpredictable behavior of the shooter and the potential for serious harm create sheer terror among everyone in the vicinity. The best strategy for developing responses to an active shooter incident is to consult local public safety personnel for recommended practices. Unfortunately, shooting incidents happen, and they must be planned for. Implications of relatively recent events involving active shooters at the University of Texas in Austin and Virginia Tech are discussed in other chapters.

Impact of the Northridge Earthquake at California State University

Susan Curzon, then Dean of the Library for California State University, reflected on the damage in an interview with Robin Featherstone:

> The collection survived but rescue work was necessary because of rain and debris damage. It was very hard going for a long time to find all of our personnel, rescue the collection, restore what services we could, set up temporary buildings, work on our new building, and document, document for FEMA [Federal Emergency Management Agency]. Some of our staff members were also in very difficult circumstances with loss of their homes or considerable damage. . . . I think in looking back that we do need to recognize post-traumatic stress more—it is far more powerful than people realize. I think the campus started back too early; people should have been given time to get their homes and families in order.

(Wilson, 2007)

Planning for Events with No Warning

Incidents that occur without warning can produce intense fear and unpredictable behavior. In August 2011, a 5.9-magnitude earthquake struck in central Virginia and was felt throughout much of the Mid-Atlantic. Because earthquakes are not common in this area, people responded to the shaking in different ways. Some sought cover, some ran from buildings; some took charge, some looked for guidance; some made good decisions, some did not. It is therefore important to frequently drill employees on proper response. At minimum the incidents can cause damage to library facilities and in worst-case scenarios can result in injury and death. A burst water pipe, for instance, can flood a nearby space without any notice and cause extensive damage. In January 2008, in just 18 minutes, over 11,000 gallons of water poured onto the second floor of the Renne Library at Montana State University in Bozeman, damaging thousands of materials, which had to be sent to a freeze-drying facility in Texas. The cost of the freeze-drying, paid for by insurance, was approximately $29,000. Unfortunately, this was the second flooding incident at the Renne Library, both caused by a burst pipe. The first incident, which had occurred a week earlier, damaged nearly 250 items in the special collections area. Smaller in number, but greater in value, the special collections materials took much longer to restore (Pettinger, 2008). If prepared for nothing else, a library should be prepared for water damage. Preparation activities include ensuring that plastic sheeting is available and that highly valued materials are appropriately marked in order to expedite proper rescue.

Earthquakes are likely the most terrifying of all disasters. Although not as frequent as hurricanes, they can be very destructive, as witnessed in Haiti, Chile, New Zealand, and Japan in 2010 and 2011. In 1994, a 6.7-magnitude earthquake damaged the library at California State University in Northridge.

As you write your service continuity plan, be cognizant of post-traumatic stress, and remember that everyone handles traumatic situations differently. Build in redundancy whenever possible so that more than one person can perform an important function.

In today's world, cyberterrorism is something that cannot be overlooked or downplayed. Cyberterrorism can produce many different kinds of threats to your library, including long-term disruptions to power and Internet connectivity. Many articles and reports have been written about the vulnerability of the electrical power grid in the United States. R. James Woolsey, Central Intelligence Agency (CIA) Director under President Clinton, testified to Congress that "it would be hard to intentionally design an electricity delivery system more vulnerable and fragile than the one on which the United States presently relies" (Trabish, 2011). As a result of the potential for a major power outage, it is essential that all libraries take this threat seriously, develop plans for days without power, and be aware of emergency power plans at the parent institution.

Designing Drills to Assist in Training for Response

Well-developed emergency response plans are of little use if members of the library staff are not well trained. One of the best ways to familiarize staff with response procedures is to perform a tabletop exercise (TTE), during which the participants respond to a designated scenario through role-play.

The TTE on the following pages can be adapted to any environment and adjusted to include other scenarios. For instance, this could be a scenario for a tornado: *Yesterday at 4:55 p.m., an EF3 tornado touched down near your library and caused structural damage, including broken windows. Electrical power is off and the library will likely be closed for five days. Hospitals in your area are currently treating a large number of people who have been wounded, and some deaths have been reported.*

Tabletop Exercise

Preparing for the Exercise

Invite to the exercise everyone who has responsibility for providing access, services, and/or resources to your patrons. Emphasize that their attendance and participation is essential.

1. Arrange for someone to take notes at the meeting for documenting any issues that arise and listing anything that needs to be worked out.
2. Make a copy of a map showing your library and the surrounding area, about a 20-mile radius.
3. Before the exercise begins, prepare slips of paper labeled "Power" and "No power" so that there will be one for each person attending the meeting. Seventy percent of the slips should say "Power" and 30 percent should say "No power." (This exercise can also be used in a pandemic or epidemic scenario where 30 percent of the slips would say "Sick.")

Scenario

In two days, a severe storm (winter storm or hurricane) is predicted to have a major impact on your area. Authorities are predicting the potential for widespread power outages, and there is a strong possibility that the library will be closed or experience disruption of services.

Conducting the Exercise

1. Pass the map around the room and ask everyone to initial the approximate place on the map where they live. Anyone who has a generator at home should circle his or her initials on the map.

2. Review the scenario with the group so that everyone understands the details of the event as it will most likely unfold. Answer any questions before beginning the response.

3. Moderate a discussion to determine which library services and resources need to be maintained in this scenario. If a Service Continuity Pocket Response Plan (described fully in chapter 4) has been completed, these resources will already be specified.

4. Determine how these core services and resources will be maintained from off-site if the library is closed.

5. Scenario 1: Pass around the container holding the paper slips and ask each attendee to take one and announce whether he or she has power or does not have power at home.

6. Discuss how the plan changes based on which staff members do and do not have power at home. Use this exercise to determine backup strategies for all core services and resources.

7. Scenario 2: Place the slips of paper back into the container and pass the container around again; for this scenario, announce that the library is now without power in addition to certain staff members not having power at home.

8. Determine strategies to implement in this scenario.

Questions for Discussion

Following are questions that may help guide the discussion. Adapt and add your own questions as needed.

1. If the library reopens while some staff are still without power at home, which staff are considered essential to report to work?

2. How will communication with essential and nonessential staff be handled?

3. Are there any library events in the next three or four days that might need to be cancelled? How will participants be contacted?

4. If the library is closed or its hours are changed because of an emergency, how will patrons be informed? Can announcements be posted to the library's website from remote locations?

5. Who is designated to communicate information through social networking tools such as Facebook and Twitter?

6. Are any books, journals, or equipment vulnerable to potential flooding?

7. Are any unique or hard-to-replace resources at risk because of potential flooding?

8. If necessary, is there another library that you could partner with to continue providing essential services or resources?

9. Are there any workplace policies that need to be considered, such as permitting staff members to work from home if the library is closed?

After-Action Review

An after-action review (AAR) is critical for identifying successes and deficiencies for a particular response. To perform AARs, it is essential to develop some kind of reporting structure. The report should feature such elements as date and time of incident, staff responding to the incident, outside agencies involved (police, fire, facilities, etc.), and actions taken. Keep the AAR as informal as possible and set ground rules that clearly specify that the purpose of the review is to improve the response system and not to place blame. As a matter of course, staff should expect an AAR within 48 hours after an incident. Careful note-taking should be part of the structure of the AAR, and all procedural changes resulting from the review should be implemented within seven days.

Conclusion

In this chapter, response actions were grouped based on the amount of notification time in order to simplify development of procedures. In addition, the importance of drills was discussed with particular emphasis on the use of tabletop exercises to reinforce essential skills. And remember, emergency situations are very stressful and can rattle even the most composed person if he or she is not adequately prepared.

To assist you with developing or enhancing your response procedures, table 2.2 provides a model based on the Emergency Response Table used at the University of Virginia Claude Moore Health Sciences Library. Adapt the table to your environment, and then post it in a very prominent location. Instruct response staff to refer to the table for all emergency situations and make changes as needed. Always remember that one of the most effective preparedness activities is vigilance—being continually aware of the potential for emergency situations and disasters and incorporating risk assessment into all ongoing planning.

We live in a world of many risks that should be dealt with proactively rather than reactively. A proactive approach includes carefully thought-out procedures for responding to a threat, accompanied by regular drills in order to incorporate what's often referred to as "muscle memory," or motor learning, and a commitment to TTEs and AARs.

TABLE 2.2 Emergency Response Table

Type of Emergency	First Response	Next Response
Active shooter	Call 911. Secure the immediate area: close doors, cover windows where possible, silence cell phones, take cover behind protective structures.	If possible without being seen by the assailant, place signs to responders in building windows, notifying them of your presence. If there is a safe route for escape, leave the area.
Bomb threat	Get as much information as possible—location of the device, when it will go off, what it looks like, why it was placed, etc. Call 911.	Report all information to your supervisor. Move to safety and await instructions from supervisor and police.
Earthquake	Protect yourself by getting underneath a sturdy table or desk. Stay inside until shaking has stopped.	Survey resulting damage, take action to safely leave the building, and assist others. Call 911 if emergency assistance is needed.
Evacuation of building	Notify all in the building to evacuate using the nearest exit. Use the PA system if power is on. Use the bullhorn to notify if power is off.	Check all areas of the building. Call 911 if emergency assistance is needed. Go to the designated assembly area, and account for coworkers. Report any absentees and where their departments are located.
Explosion	Call 911 and initiate evacuation of the building.	Report to responders if any injured remain in the building.
Fire	Call 911, and pull the nearest fire alarm if not already activated. Evacuate the building.	Contain fire by closing doors. Move persons with limited mobility to a safe area in a stairwell. Use fire extinguisher (pull pin; aim; squeeze handle; sweep from side to side) if deemed effective.
Flood	Call facilities management. Do not walk into standing water!	Use water-absorbent socks to block water or absorb seeping water. Cover library collections or furniture with plastic sheeting.
Hazardous materials spill	Move away from the spill, and block access to it.	Call facilities management to clean up the spill. Call 911 if emergency service is required because of contamination.

(Continued)

TABLE 2.2 Emergency Response Table *(Continued)*

Type of Emergency	First Response	Next Response
Hostage	Call 911. Clear the area to avoid others becoming hostages; move to a safe area (behind a door or a solid wall).	Report all pertinent information to responders (police or other).
Medical emergency	Call 911. Give the location of the emergency; follow directions from the 911 operator.	Use the PA system to request assistance from any doctor or nurse in the building. Stay with the victim until help arrives.
Power outage	Call facilities management and ask if there is any information about the cause or duration of the outage.	If the power is off for longer than 15 minutes, or if it is dark outside when the power goes off, initiate closing procedures immediately. Check elevators to see if anyone is stranded. Check all areas of the library for patrons who need help; take flashlights to assist people to leave if the building is dark. Once the library is closed, lock the front doors. Supervisor reports immediately to library management. Stay nearby to await restoration of power or until notified by library management that the library will remain closed.
Severe weather	During heavy rains, check flood/leak-prone areas in the building for water.	Contact a library manager to find out whether to close the library based on existing circumstances.
Tornado	*Watch:* monitor weather reporting stations online. *Warning:* announce that the warning is posted; use the PA to instruct everyone to move away from windows.	If a tornado warning is issued for the city, ask patrons to move away from windows and exterior doors and to move as low in the building as possible.

References

American Library Association (ALA). 2011. "Pandemic Planning." ALA. Last modified March 18. http://wikis.ala.org/professionaltips/index.php/Pandemic_Planning.

Pettinger, Anne. 2008. "Once Damaged by Flooding, Dried Books Return to MSU Library." *Montana State University News*, March 19. http://www.montana.edu/news/5705/once-damaged-by-flooding-dried-books-return-to-msu-library.

Trabish, Herman K. 2011. "Cyber-Attacks, Attacks on the Grid, Electromagnetic Pulses, and Geomagnetic Storms, Oh My!" greentechmedia. June 3. http://www.greentechmedia.com/articles/read/cyber-attacks-attacks-on-the-grid-electromagnetic-pulses-and-geomagnetic-st.

Wilson, Daniel T. 2007. "University Library for California State University, Northridge." NN/LM Emergency Preparedness and Response Toolkit. National Network of Libraries of Medicine. Posted June 27. http://nnlm.gov/ep/2007/06/27/library-disaster-stories-northridge-earthquake/.

———. 2008. "Library Disaster Story: Hurricane Dolly." NN/LM Emergency Preparedness and Response Toolkit. National Network of Libraries of Medicine. Posted December 12, 2008. http://nnlm.gov/ep/2008/12/12/library-disaster-story-hurricane-dolly.

Wisconsin Department of Public Instruction. 2014. "Pandemic Flu Planning for Wisconsin Public Libraries." Wisconsin Department of Public Instruction. Accessed March 26. http://pld.dpi.wi.gov/pld_pandemic.

Woolsey, Matt. 2008. "America's Most Expensive Natural Disasters." Forbes.com. September 13. http://www.forbes.com/2007/10/29/property-disaster-hurricane-forbeslife-cx_mw_1029disaster.html.

World Health Organization (WHO). 2010. "H1N1 in Post-pandemic Period." WHO. December 11. http://www.who.int/mediacentre/news/statements/2010/h1n1_vpc_20100810/en/index.html.

From Self-Reliance to Asking for Help

Chance never helps those that do not help themselves.

—Sophocles

IN THIS CHAPTER:

✓ On-Site Planning

✓ Off-Site Planning

✓ Outside Assistance Planning

✓ Conclusion

✓ References

This chapter is designed to provide a background and structure for three important elements of disaster planning: on-site planning, off-site planning, and obtaining outside assistance. Gaining knowledge of these three elements is essential in disaster planning and, like all areas of planning, requires accurate documentation and diligent updating. They also play a key role when creating a one-page disaster plan, which chapter 4 addresses in detail.

It is good business practice to be self-sufficient. Policies and procedures are written to ensure a smooth-running operation, so minor incidents and service disruptions are handled without difficulty. Parent institutions and communities where libraries reside are also designed to be self-reliant, and if something happens to compromise that self-reliance, a local structure is in place to deal with the disruption. Support from a parent institution or community is part of a support infrastructure built on local, regional, state, and national assistance. This structure, known as the National Response Framework (NRF), contains principles on how to respond before, during, and after a crisis.

Within the NRF is the National Information Management System (NIMS), which provides a set of processes that enable collaborative incident management. Whereas NRF presents the structure, NIMS guides how everyone connected to emergency preparedness and response communicates with one another. Further discussion of NIMS is included in chapter 7.

Everyone connected to an emergency services–related discipline is required, at minimum, to take FEMA IS-700.A, "National Incident Management System (NIMS) An Introduction," and IS-100.B, "Introduction to Incident Command System, ICS-100." All librarians with preparedness and response duties should take these two courses, which are self-paced and available on the FEMA website (http://fema.gov/) at no cost.

All preparedness and response planning is predicated on providing assistance once local resources have been exhausted. One of the many goals

The National Response Framework

"The National Response Framework presents the guiding principles that enable all response partners to prepare for and provide a unified national response to disasters and emergencies—from the smallest incident to the largest catastrophe.

"The Framework defines the key principles, roles, and structures that organize the way we respond as a Nation. It describes how communities, tribes, States, the Federal Government, and private-sector and nongovernmental partners apply these principles for a coordinated, effective national response. It also identifies special circumstances where the Federal Government exercises a larger role, including incidents where Federal interests are involved and catastrophic incidents where a State would require significant support. The Framework enables first responders, decision makers, and supporting entities to provide a unified national response."

(Homeland Security, 2008)

of this book is to build the same kind of response structures in libraries as those which are practiced by municipalities. This translates to stockpiling response supplies on-site, having a service continuity plan designed to keep core services and resources available following some kind of service disruption, and having a contingency plan for obtaining outside assistance once local resources are exhausted. Basically, you are building a protective shell around your physical library and its virtual components.

There will come a time when even the most prepared library will need outside assistance. This will happen when a local infrastructure is totally compromised because of an extreme natural event, such as a hurricane, tornado, or earthquake, or a man-made event, such as an act of terrorism. However, libraries can apply strategies to extend their ability to provide core resources and services.

On-Site Planning

Cross-Training

Libraries should begin with a strong commitment to cross-training. Many libraries have already implemented cross-training to maintain library services, most often to compensate for short staffing. A closer look at cross-training provides insight into the *genesis* of disaster planning. To ensure a successful cross-training program, all procedures need to be written down and regularly updated, a process similar to maintaining any disaster plan. With procedures written down and centrally available to all staff, many threats to a service disruption can be assuaged or even thwarted. Documenting work flow and making the documentation accessible to those affiliated with the library are now easier with the use of an intranet. However, be cognizant of not relying only on a functioning intranet for cross-training documentation. Because power outages are a major cause of service disruptions and can accompany many different types of events, build in redundancy by either printing documentation or downloading it to a device with backup power.

Once cross-training procedures are in place and practiced, advance to the next level by developing procedures for staffing the library with a single staff member. Of course, those libraries that are already staffed by solo librarians are ahead of the game.

Libraries with two or more staff should develop a one-person plan by arranging a meeting with stakeholders and creating a document detailing how one person can maintain essential services, regardless of the library's size. At the meeting, determine which essential services can be maintained by one person. Keep in mind that the person available may not be familiar with the provision of these services, so all procedures should be clearly spelled out. The plan should begin with procedures for how to open the library and end with closing procedures. In between, list procedures for providing the most important services. To illustrate what this document might look like, the following is a sample document from a large academic health sciences library. Note the liberal referrals to other documentation, a necessary ingredient in this kind of planning.

Flying Solo

Should you find yourself the only staff person present at the Library, outlined here are services identified as being most important to patrons, with instructions for providing them on a limited basis.

Entering the library and checking in with management

- Use your ID to get into the library.
- If the card key system is not operating or if you don't have your ID with you, dial "0" on one of the phones in the hallway and ask for Security. Request that someone meet you at the main entrance to let you in. Once inside the Library, if no one from the Library Service Desk is here, verify that the library has not been officially closed by calling the main library phone number and checking the voicemail message.

Opening procedures

Find the copy of the *Service Desk Quick Reference* manual that is available on the Library's intranet and also shelved in print at the Service Desk. Locate "Opening Procedures" (contents of the manual are arranged alphabetically by title) and follow the steps.

If there is not time to do everything on the Opening Procedures list before opening proceed in this order

- Turn on all the lights on the main floor.
- Unlock public rooms.
- Return to the lobby and go downstairs; turn on lights in the public areas.
- Open the library's front doors.
- Come back to the Library Service Desk and do the rest of the opening functions (see the *Service Desk Quick Reference* manual).

Helping patrons at the Library Service Desk

- The Service Desk is to be staffed whenever the Library is open.
- If you are the only one here and you are not a member of the Service Desk staff, you can still provide basic patron services by following the procedures in the *Service Desk Quick Reference* manual.

Document delivery requests (borrowing procedures)

- Locate the "ILL Procedures" section in the *Service Desk Quick Reference* manual. Follow the instructions listed for each function.

Historical Collections

Historical Collections will not be open to the public during times of limited staffing, unless otherwise directed by the head of Historical Collections. If there should be an urgent request for materials in Historical Collections from the School of Medicine, the School of Nursing, and so forth, contact the head of Historical Collections at home using the directory found at the end of the *Service Desk Quick Reference* manual. Remember that you can contact Library staff members at home whenever necessary by using the directory at the end of the *Service Desk Quick Reference* manual.

Closing the Library

If you are directed to close the Library, closing procedures are included in the *Service Desk Quick Reference* manual. Most importantly when closing:

- Make sure everyone has left the Library (check bathrooms).
- Close the entrance doors.
- Turn off the lights, and lock the public rooms.
- Make sure the main entrance doors lock behind you when you leave.

Good work! I'm sure our patrons appreciated your efforts!

> *–Susan Yowell*
> *Circulation Manager*
> *University of Virginia Claude Moore Health Sciences Library*
> *Charlottesville, VA*

Prevention

Prevention is another important strategy that libraries can incorporate to help minimize service disruptions and closings. Most people have heard the Benjamin Franklin quote "An ounce of prevention is worth a pound of cure." Put this quote into practice as you take steps toward becoming better prepared. Here are a few areas to consider (contact local emergency planners for additional information):

- Prevention of illness
- Prevention of fire
- Prevention of flooding and water leaks
- Prevention of loss of connectivity

Prevention of Illness

Preventing the spread of disease is a good starting point. As a result of the H1N1 pandemic of 2009, most libraries are better equipped to respond to an epidemic or pandemic. Employees are encouraged to get a flu shot, and some institutions even bring in qualified health professionals to administer shots in their facilities. Hand sanitizers are now common in libraries, and patrons are more aware of the need to clean their hands following contact with shared equipment, such as keyboards, mice, and remotes. In addition, many libraries have adjusted their approach to sick leave, now requiring staff to stay home if they are sick and not report to work until they are no longer contagious. During the H1N1 pandemic the Centers for Disease Control and Prevention (CDC, 2009) recommended that employees not return to work until 24 hours after their fever abated without using fever-reducing drugs. These are positive steps and important weapons in combating future spread of disease.

In summary, here is a list of four steps all libraries can take to prevent the spread of illness:

1. Take advantage of flu vaccination programs.
2. Use antibacterial hand cleaners, especially staff who are in contact with the public at the service desk.
3. Use disinfectant wipes at the service desk for the telephones, keyboards, and computer mice.
4. Ask staff who are sick to stay home rather than coming to work and possibly infecting others.

Prevention of Fire

Libraries, filled with combustible materials and open to the public, are particularly vulnerable to fire. Fires can be accidental, such as a faulty wire, or intentional, such as arson, civil strife, mob violence, or warfare. No matter how it originates, a fire can quickly destroy a building and all its contents. Fortunately, most libraries today adhere to strict fire codes, greatly reducing the possibility of an accidental fire. In addition, many libraries provide fire extinguisher training for staff to increase the likelihood a fire will be extinguished before it gets out of control.

Prevention of Flooding and Water Leaks

Flooding, like fire, has always been a major threat to libraries. Flooding can come in many forms and can occur when least expected. River flooding, clogged drains, frozen pipes, poorly maintained HVAC units, and even overflowing toilets can cause major damage. To help prevent flooding, be cognizant of the environment surrounding the library and be especially diligent when construction is happening in or around the facility. Because flooding can be caused by many scenarios, always have plastic sheeting on hand as well as other equipment needed to respond to a water situation.

Prevention of Loss of Connectivity

In today's world, patrons count on libraries to provide access to the Internet and online materials purchased or leased by the library. According to the report *Opportunity for All: How the American Public Benefits from Internet Access at U.S. Libraries*, "77 million (32 percent) Americans age 14 or older took advantage of Internet access in a public library" in 2009 (Becker et al., 2010: 32). The report goes on to point out that low-income adults are particularly reliant on library Internet access, stating that "44 percent of people living in households below the federal poverty line ($22,000 a year for a family of four) used public library computers and the Internet access" (Becker et al., 2010: 2). This is particularly the case in health care, where a large number of adults regularly search the Internet for health-related information, and many health-care workers rely on online resources. Libraries that house or provide access to any critical information that might be

Construction Situation at the University of Iowa

Nondisasters can also create the need to provide services off-site. In the summer of 2011, the Hardin Library of the Health Sciences at the University of Iowa in Iowa City underwent major construction. Library staff devised a service plan that included sites around campus, since access to the library was restricted. Following is their services plan:

- Two temporary locations will be set up where library users can pick up materials and consult with staff. One location will be in MERF (375 Newton Rd.) in the atrium and will be open 7:30 a.m.–6:00 p.m., Monday–Friday, and 1:00–5:00 p.m., Sunday. Simulation Center equipment, laptop checkouts, and much of the reserve book collection will also be relocated to 1155 MERF and available Monday–Friday.
- A second library location will be situated in the Pharmacy Building Computer Lab (115 South

Continued on p. 39

needed following a major services disruption have a responsibility to ensure a backup power plan is in place for times when the power goes down. The ideal backup system is a generator that kicks on when the main power is compromised and continues to run until power is restored. These backup power systems are usually found only where power is critical to the survival of the institution, such as at a campus computer center or a hospital. If the library is affiliated with either a university or a hospital, you might be able to work out an arrangement to have core servers housed where a backup power system is available. More libraries will have access to these systems in the future if the provision of emergency backup power becomes standard for all new construction.

Off-Site Planning

Off-site planning focuses on the provision of core services from a site, or sites, away from the library. These remote sites could be another campus location or, more likely in an emergency situation, at a staff member's home.

Service disruptions from tornadoes, flooding, riots, illness, severe winter weather, and transportation problems can all create a scenario where services are best provided remotely, and as technology blurs the line between home and work, it creates new possibilities for service continuity. Libraries that already allow telecommuting have procedures in place and therefore have a head start on other libraries. Libraries that do not permit telecommuting should at least consider a day or two per year for staff who maintain core services to work from home, as this practice is essential for determining technology needs from a remote site. Core services that can be performed at home include interlibrary loan, reference assistance, and troubleshooting access problems to core online materials. Begin by looking at these services, and then expand or pull back based on the library's mission and clients' needs. Please note that it is important to consult with the human resources department to determine if institutional policies prevent library staff from working remotely.

All library staff who have a role in providing core resources and services from a remote site should meet regularly to review procedures, check availability of recovery equipment and supplies, and test all communication channels, including information for staff and the public. Should the likelihood of a service disruption exist, someone should determine team members' availability and quickly establish backup coverage for anyone who will not be available. A stable communication system is critical, and redundancy must be built in to execute your plan, such as a primary system with two backup means if the primary system is compromised. It is advisable to include home and cell numbers as well as an alternative e-mail address, such as a Google or Yahoo account, in the contact information for all participants.

Outside Assistance Planning

When a major service disruption exhausts local resources, outside assistance will be needed. Potential sources of outside assistance include the following:

- Backup library
- Library networks and conservation centers
- Commercial salvage and recovery companies

Backup Library

A backup library, located either inside or outside a library system, can be called on to assist in the delivery of core resources and services. Again, every library, no matter its size, should examine core services, create local redundancy plans, and then apply the remote aspects to a backup library. Clearly, the number of services that can be provided decreases as you advance from on-site planning to a backup library, often because of licensing restrictions. However, in recent large natural disasters, many library vendors have been willing to provide access to their content to aid in disaster recovery so contact your vendors after a disaster. Generally, the core services that might fit best in an arrangement with a backup library are reference services, such as Ask a Librarian chat, and interlibrary loan. In some cases, depending on the affiliation of the backup library and its proximity, access to online resources and even instructional space can be included in the agreement.

To find a backup library, begin by developing an arrangement with a library that you regularly work with, either in a consortium or within the same system. This will facilitate working out backup procedures because an established working relationship already exists. Once a backup plan is developed, look for a library outside your region and implement a similar plan. A good rule of thumb is to eventually develop a backup arrangement with a library in another power grid and in a different geographic area. You can find power interconnections and regions by doing an image search in your browser using the terms *NERC* (North American Electric Reliability Corporation) and *Power Grid*.

Libraries developing a backup plan with another library can use the model memorandum of understanding (MOU) provided by the New Jersey Hospital Association and adapt it to local needs (see figure 3.1).

A great example of a library network using this MOU is the aid agreement between the academic health sciences libraries at the University of North Carolina, Duke, Wake Forest, Eastern Carolina University, and hospitals in different regions of the North Carolina Area Health Education Center (AHEC). The agreement, developed in 2010, has an oversight committee and was signed by all library directors in participating libraries. In advance of Hurricane Irene, which went up the Eastern Seaboard in August 2011, the MOU was activated and its primary communication mechanism, a dedicated electronic discussion list, was tested, as was the backup

Continued from p. 38

Grand Ave.) and will be open 7:30 a.m.–5:00 p.m., Monday–Friday. Computers and printing will be available to all users.

- Library patrons will be able to request books from the Hardin collection using InfoHawk's Request feature. Because staff will only be able to enter the building once per day, it may take as long as two days for materials to be pulled. Requested material can be delivered to offices via campus mail or can be picked up at one of the temporary locations or at another UI library.
- Books checked out to faculty, graduate/professional students, and undergraduate honors students which are currently due in June 2011 will be automatically renewed until June 2012. An e-mail will be sent to users whose books are automatically renewed. Please be aware that this applies only to books checked out from Hardin Library on long-term loans.

(Lawrence, 2011)

Participating libraries

_____

_____

_____

_____

Purpose

The purpose of this Memorandum of Understanding (MOU) is to establish a framework through which participating libraries might endeavor to assist one another following a disaster that exceeds the response capability of an affected library. The MOU outlines the ways personnel, services, and communications can be conducted in times of emergencies such that an affected library would be supported in its efforts to provide needed and/or essential information for its users, clients, and patrons.

Through this MOU, no library is committed to provide specific services or to offer aid that exceeds its resources and abilities as determined by that library in its sole discretion. Generally, the parties intend a framework of speedy initial assistance for a period that would not exceed seven (7) days. That period could be extended if agreed upon by the partnering library or libraries.

Definition of a disaster

A disaster is an occurrence such as a hurricane, tornado, storm, flood, high water, earthquake, drought, blizzard, pestilence, famine, fire, explosion, building collapse, transportation wreck, terrorist event, bioterrorist event, pandemic, power failure, or other similar natural or man-made incident(s).

Method of cooperation

On a biannual basis (recommended dates: on or near the first day of spring and the first day of winter) the partner libraries will update each other regarding any changes related to this MOU. The participants may also amend this MOU to better reflect their mutual understandings and commitments at that time.

Responsibilities of the library partners

Activation/warning/communications

The following items should be completed as agreed to by the partner libraries and detailed below and/or with an attached Addendum (if more space is needed). Determine how and when to request activation of support during a disaster or if there is a need to advise a partner there may be a need to activate, depending upon weather or other warning systems.

Whom to contact

(Include staff tree, names, titles, and/or alternates.)

_____

_____

_____

(Continued)

FIGURE 3.1 Memorandum of Understanding *(Continued)*

How to contact

(Include phone tree, cell phones, addresses, fax, e-mail, and indication of home or office information.)

_____

_____

_____

Services offered

(Check all that apply and specify definitions, parameters, or limits, if any, on attached page.)

❑ Interlibrary Loan

❑ Ask a Librarian/Chat

❑ Online Resources Support

❑ Other: _____

❑ Other: _____

Cost recovery

The partnering libraries agree that each will cover any costs associated with its delivery of support or aid to another partner and that each, therefore, has the sole discretion to determine what resources and support it can provide to another library in the event of a covered disaster.

Signature	**Signature**
Print name	**Print name**
Title	**Title**
Library	**Library**
Institution	**Institution**
Address	**Address**
Date	**Date**

Source: http://nnlm.gov/sea/services/emergency/modelmou.pdf.

communication system. Following the event all libraries reported their status and help was initiated where needed. The backup system developed by the North Carolina libraries is quite impressive and could serve as a model for other states and networks.

Setting Up a Backup System

In the winter of 2008, the Health Sciences Library at the University of North Carolina in Chapel Hill and the Claude Moore Health Sciences Library at the University of Virginia in Charlottesville developed a backup system for keeping their interlibrary loan (ILL) services functioning despite staff availability. The arrangement originated at a time when the H1N1 virus was spreading worldwide and there was a real potential for a pandemic. Both libraries had developed plans for providing ILL from a home location, but they had not addressed the scenario where interlibrary loan staff members were too sick to carry out their duties from home, as might be the case in a pandemic.

The plan was quite simple but required the same ILL management system, in this case ILLiad. Here is how the plan worked. If staff members from either of the libraries were too sick to carry out ILL transactions from home, a call for assistance can be made to the backup library's ILL department. Within minutes, staff at the backup library would "take over" a dedicated workstation at the affected library and carry out ILL borrowing requests in a process that is seamless to patrons. Both institutions agreed that no costs would be incurred, and there would be no reimbursement of staff time during the agreed-on length of provision. Only borrowing requests would be processed; lending requests would be suspended and therefore routed on to the next library. Testing of the plan has taken place with positive outcomes. Both libraries talk regularly to keep procedures and contact information up-to-date. To be adapted at other libraries, though, it is essential that all parties are cooperative, flexible, and willing to share IP addresses.

–Daniel T. Wilson
Associate Director, Collection Management and Access Services
University of Virginia Claude Moore Health Sciences Library
Charlottesville, VA

Library Networks and Conservation Centers

Although there is a plethora of national, state, and local relief agencies available to libraries following a major service disruption, a few promote their services specifically to libraries or related institutions, such as museums. Some of these agencies are discussed here; many more are included in the appendix.

Amigos Library Services

Amigos Library Services is a nonprofit, membership-based organization in Dallas, Texas, serving primarily the South Central and Southwest United States. Amigos offers guidance in the event of an emergency through its Imaging and Preservation Service.

LYRASIS

LYRASIS is a nonprofit, membership-based organization in Atlanta, Georgia, serving states in the Southeast, Mid-Atlantic, and New England regions. Through its Digital and Preservation Services division LYRASIS offers assistance to libraries that have suffered damage. For libraries located within the continental United States, LYRASIS may be able to arrange for a volunteer to help with the response and recovery process.

WESTPAS

WESTPAS (Western States and Territories Preservation Assistance Service) is a regional library and archives preservation service, serving states primarily in the Northwest and West United States. Phone consultation is provided at no charge, and on-site assistance can be arranged.

Northeast Document Conservation Center

The Northeast Document Conservation Center (NEDCC) is a nonprofit, regional conservation center out of Andover, Massachusetts. NEDCC provides telephone advice and referrals but no on-site assistance.

National Network of Libraries of Medicine

The National Network of Libraries of Medicine (NN/LM), coordinated by the National Library of Medicine (NLM), has as its mission "to advance the progress of medicine and improve the public health by providing all U.S. health professionals with equal access to biomedical information and improving the public's access to information to enable them to make informed decisions about their health" (National Network of Libraries of Medicine, 2012). In 2006, in response to the profound impact of hurricanes Katrina and Rita on our health system, NLM charged NN/LM to strengthen its network's emergency response system by establishing more extensive disaster response plans. As a result, in January 2008, after soliciting help from national experts, NN/LM implemented its National Emergency Preparedness and Response Initiative. The initiative is designed to help mitigate the impact of disasters on health-care providers and the public by creating robust preparedness and response capabilities and building a backup system to be employed when local resources break down or are exhausted. The primary resource for assistance in both preparedness and response is the NN/LM National Emergency Preparedness and Response (EP&R) Toolkit.

NN/LM Emergency Preparedness and Response Toolkit

The NN/LM EP&R Toolkit has three primary functions: serve as a warehouse of emergency preparedness and response documentation, such as plans and tabletop exercises, that can be downloaded and adapted to any environment; link to other resources that promote preparedness and response activities; and archive current news stories about the direct impact or related impact of disasters on library services.

Emergency Access Initiative

The Emergency Access Initiative (EAI) is the result of a partnership between the NLM, the NN/LM, the Professional/Scholarly Publishing Division of the Association of American Publishers, and other publishers. EAI provides full-text access to biomedical literature to aid health-care practitioners, librarians, and the general public anywhere in the world following a major disaster. For more localized disasters that are too small in scale to warrant EAI activation, libraries should check with publishers and describe their needs for emergency access. As some of the library stories shared in chapter 6 reflect, publishers have been generous to libraries faced with emergency situations to ensure that communities have the information they need. In some cases, publishers have made content on specific topics available for free, as demonstrated by publisher responses to the H1N1 crisis, or when the *New York Times* took down its pay wall for all Hurricane Irene–related news.

American Library Association

The American Library Association (ALA) website has links to many preparedness and response resources. Particularly relevant to this chapter is a page titled "Helping United States Libraries After Disasters" (American Library Association, 2014). The page lists states with libraries currently needing assistance and provides contact information for international efforts, such as those in Haiti, Chile, and Japan.

Commercial Salvage and Recovery Companies

Commercial salvage and recovery companies are often used by libraries following a significant event that damages print collections. These companies will typically send a representative, free of charge, to assess the damaged materials and discuss options. Service agreements are also available for libraries with extremely valuable materials that might need priority treatment following a large-scale disaster.

BELFOR

BELFOR advertises that it can handle "the smallest medical record to an entire library system." They have large-capacity freeze-drying chambers in areas around the country and mobile units available to respond to a disaster. BELFOR has a very nice website that lists its emergency number and includes an interactive map of the United States that quickly provides specific state company locations.

Blackmon-Mooring-Steamatic Catastrophe, Inc. (BMS-CAT)

BMS-CAT advertises that they can "recover a range of data—plain documentation, paper, journals, books, records, film, libraries, archives, historical archives, and magnetic media—that years ago would have been considered a total loss." Its website also features an emergency number and a seasonal hurricane tracker from the Weather Underground.

Conclusion

This chapter outlined methods for libraries to be more self-sufficient and better prepared for any kind of service disruption. In addition, it included steps libraries can take to facilitate outside assistance from a variety of sources in the event that local resources and plans become inoperable. Always remember that although disasters are local, there are plenty of resources available to you either arranged in advance or on an as-needed basis.

References

American Library Association (ALA). 2014. "Helping United States Libraries." ALA. Accessed March 26. http://www.ala.org/offices/cro/getinvolved/helpinglibraries.

Becker, Samantha, Michael D. Crandall, Karen E. Fisher, Bo Kinney, Carol Landry, and Anita Rocha. 2010. *Opportunity for All: How the American Public Benefits from Internet Access at U.S. Libraries* (IMLS-2010-RES-01). Washington, DC: Institute of Museum and Library Services.

Centers for Disease Control and Prevention (CDC). 2009. "CDC Recommendations for the Amount of Time Persons with Influenza-Like Illness Should Be Away from Others." CDC. October 23. http://www.cdc.gov/h1n1flu/guidance/exclusion.htm.

Homeland Security. 2008. "Introducing . . . National Response Framework." Federal Emergency Management Association. http://www.fema.gov/pdf/emergency/nrf/about_nrf.pdf.

Lawrence, Janna. 2011. "More News about Hardin's Summer Plans." *Hardin Library Staff, News, Services* (blog), May 1. http://blog.lib.uiowa.edu/hardin/2011/05/01/more-news-about-hardins-summer-plans/.

National Network of Libraries of Medicine (NN/LM). 2012. "About the National Network of Libraries of Medicine (NN/LM)." NN/LM. Last updated January 30. http://nnlm.gov/about/.

A One-Page Service Continuity Plan

4

On Saturday, June 4, 2010, a microburst struck Dry Springs, Ohio, at 2:34 p.m. (A microburst is a severe storm that produces straight-line winds, often in excess of 70 miles per hour. Think of it as a storm that approaches like a tornado but has the effect of a hurricane.) The Dry Springs Public Library was severely damaged when a limb snapped off a large oak tree and punctured a hole in the west end of the roof. Wind-driven rain came pouring into the gaping hole, which then began to seep into the main floor through light fixtures. Located on the main floor were current journals, the book collection, a bank of computers, a display of rare local history books, and a filing cabinet full of old letters that Joshua Landers, the founder of the town, wrote to his wife, Elizabeth, about daily life in Dry Springs while she was away from him and living in Boston.

The seeping water became a steady stream and pounded down on a range of books, splashing onto a nearby bank of computers. A second leak began to appear near the center of the room, precariously close to the rare book display. The power blinked twice and then went out.

Because it was a Saturday, only two staff members were working; Judy Mendez, the weekend supervisor, and Millie Reed, a part-time shelver. Judy grabbed plastic sheeting kept in the staff lounge and then found several patrons who were willing to help cover the books. Fortunately, two months earlier Judy had attended disaster training offered by their regional library network, so she knew that there was a risk of electrocution and instructed the volunteers to stay clear of standing water, even though the power was currently out. Once the stacks were protected, they quickly covered the computers. As she approached the display of rare local history books, Judy noticed the second leak. She quickly moved the books off the table and observed that two of them were water damaged. She kept the two separated from the other books, carefully opening them so they could dry. Most of the patrons were still in the library, so Judy turned her attention to the situation outside the library. She looked around and saw tree branches littering the front yard of the library, but otherwise it looked like it was safe, so she closed

IN THIS CHAPTER:

✓ Background

✓ Service Continuity Pocket Response Plan

✓ Conclusion

✓ References

the library and sent Millie home. Exhausted, Judy sat down at her desk and called the library director, Mary Callhoun, who had left that morning to attend a conference in Pittsburgh.

Mary listened intently as Judy retold the incident. She wished the library had power so they could establish a video call and she could see the damage. Instead, Judy walked around the floor describing everything that she saw over the phone.

Mary was concerned about the wet rare books and asked if the letters from Joshua Landers sustained any damage. Judy opened the filing cabinet and reported that all the letters were safe. Greatly relieved, Mary commended Judy for her work and asked her to stay in the library while she made some calls.

Mary reached in her purse and pulled out her one-page service continuity plan. Starting with the first column on the left, she contacted the town office and left a message that the library would be closed indefinitely. She then contacted Rich Bear, director of facilities. Rich was home and available. He said that he would head over to the library to assess the damage, take pictures, and then seal off the hole in the roof. Concerned about the rare books, Mary found the telephone number for her regional library network that offered 24/7/365 consultation for damaged books and materials. She dialed the number and spoke to Kathy Banks. Kathy listened to Mary describe the situation and then advised Mary to have someone place the two books in a freezer in order to prevent mold. She also gave Mary the numbers for a nearby commercial salvage company and a local preservationist. Mary called Judy back and relayed to her Kathy's recommendation to place the two water-damaged books in the freezer and that she would stay on the phone until Judy had done this. When Judy got back on the phone, Mary thanked her once again for her prompt actions and gave her permission to go home.

Mary then called members of her three-person disaster team and they discussed their roles. The head of information technology did not have his plan handy, so Mary sent him a PDF copy using her smartphone. The library's head of public services took on the responsibility of monitoring chat and the Ask a Librarian service. They agreed to do this only during normal library hours until the library could reopen. The collection services librarian volunteered to go to the library to check on the collections with the director of facilities. Mary, responsible for communications, got out her laptop and put closing information on the library's website, Facebook page, and Twitter feed, using the instructions on the plan. Finally, she contacted a local radio station, briefly described the situation, and left contact information if they needed to reach her. Just 68 minutes after the limb came smashing through the roof, the situation was under control, thanks to the quick actions of library staff, the perfect execution of a one-page disaster response plan, and technology.

This account is fictitious and is included to illustrate the value of a one-page response plan designed specifically for keeping core services and resources available following a major service disruption. The remainder of this chapter focuses on the steps needed to create such a plan, column by column. To help visualize the plan, information about the content in each column is accompanied by a template. The front page of the plan addresses communication and service continuity, with emphasis on the actions that should occur within the first hour of a disruption. The back page deals primarily with rescue and recovery of physical collections and lists individuals/places that can be contacted if outside assistance is needed.

Background

Writing a disaster plan is an arduous task, requiring a time commitment that most librarians feel challenged to find. To make matters worse, a disaster plan requires continual updating because an out-of-date disaster plan is of little value and may even do harm. As a result, most disaster plans are not dynamic but instead are static, housed on a shelf, out-of-sight and out-of-mind, presenting this dichotomy: something that can be so critical to the continued operation of a library and a valuable resource to a community or institution is something that is too often neglected.

This book is grounded in reality. In today's world of shrinking library budgets, positions are being eliminated and services are being cut or reduced. Remaining staff assume more responsibility, and even important tasks are moved further down the priority list or are abandoned entirely. Unfortunately, disaster planning often becomes a low-priority item continually displaced by more immediate needs.

Fortunately, libraries now have a less time-consuming option: a one-page service continuity plan. It is imperative that every library commit time to complete a one-page plan. To facilitate this endeavor, the one-page plan presented here focuses on the essentials for keeping library services and resources available following a service disruption. The template for this plan was adapted from the Pocket Response Plan (PReP) created by the Council of State Archivists, or CoSA (Council of State Archivists, 2011). The plan carries no copyright restrictions as long as any adaptation includes acknowledgment that the local plan is based on the CoSA template. CoSA specifically states on its website that the PReP is meant to complement, not replace, an agency's disaster plan; however, this adaptation can stand independently as a disaster planning and response tool. Granted, a fully thought-out and written disaster plan is important and we encourage all libraries to develop and maintain one, but if you do not have the time and/or the resources to accomplish this, creating a one-page plan like the one outlined in this chapter will be invaluable.

For the purposes of this book, the plan is called Service Continuity PReP, or SCPReP. Again, it differs from the CoSA plan in that it focuses on plans for keeping core services and resources available following a service disruption, whereas the CoSA plan concentrates on saving collections. The SCPReP does acknowledge the importance of unique and hard to replace collections, and space has been allotted to address this issue.

Service Continuity Pocket Response Plan

Traditionally, a disaster plan is something kept on-site in a large three-ring binder. Sometimes duplicates are made of the disaster plan and kept strategically off-site. In contrast, the SCPReP is designed to be mobile and available regardless of where members of your Service Continuity Team (SCT) are located (see figures 4.1 and 4.2, pp. 52–53). Contact information, response procedures, and roles are all included in the plan; therefore, all that is required is for SCT members to be accessible either by landline phone, a cell tower, or a satellite phone.

Your SCPReP should be available in both paper and electronic formats. Paper copies are great for quick study or for use when a reliable power source is not available. However, paper can be hard to replicate and distribute in an emergency, so keeping an electronic copy on a laptop or mobile device is essential (see figure 4.3, p. 54). For instance, your response coordinator might choose to send all members of the SCT a copy of the most up-to-date plan in order to ensure that everyone is working from the same document. Obviously, this does not work if all communication systems are down, which is why you want to keep the current plan in paper, in either your wallet or your purse.

Column 1: Institutional Contacts

The first column should contain institutional contacts. Include contact information for offices and individuals within the community or institution that would be notified if the library had to be closed unexpectedly. Provide alternate contact methods for each individual, including, if possible, office, home, and cell phone numbers as well as both work and personal e-mail addresses. From the perspective of an academic health sciences library, the list of contacts would likely include the Office of Risk Management, media or public affairs office, Finance and Administration, Student Affairs, Security, Facilities, and Environmental Health and Safety. Other institutional contacts would also be useful, such as the deans of the various schools and colleges the library serves and affiliated hospitals and clinics.

Column 2: Library Disaster Team Roles and Contact Information

Column 2 provides an opportunity to create a disaster team, if a team is not already in place. In its simplest form, your team is composed of the library director and managers who oversee core library services. The disaster team coordinates developing, writing, and updating the plan and executes the plan when needed. Once again, current contact information is crucial and in this case must include home, office, cell, and personal e-mail for each member of the team. In addition, include a brief description of the role each person plays following a disaster. Here are some examples:

- Library Director: Coordinates all decision making and is liaison to institutional or community agencies. Only person designated to speak to media.
- Director of Collection Management: Coordinates response activities for all collections. Is knowledgeable about strategies for saving print materials and is the liaison with library networks and commercial recovery services. Primary liaison with backup libraries.
- Director of Information Services: Coordinates planning for continuity of patron services, including chat and e-mail. Also responsible for coordinating the delivery of information services from a remote site should the library building not be habitable.
- Director of Technology: Coordinates planning strategies for dealing with all network problems, computer equipment issues, and data recovery.
- Business Services Manager: Coordinates the maintenance of telephone service, is liaison for facility issues, and handles equipment, supplies, and insurance.
- Communications: Coordinates strategies for communicating with patrons and staff.

Column 3: Communication Plan

A successful disaster plan is inextricably linked to a communications plan that must detail when to contact, whom to contact, and how to contact. Make certain that all contact information is up-to-date, communication modes are regularly checked, and redundancy is built in. Finally, include a leadership transition plan for use in the event that your library director (or person in charge) is unable to carry out his or her leadership responsibilities.

How will you notify your patrons and staff of closing information? Voice messaging? Facebook? Twitter? Website? Hopefully, you will incorporate all four. Following flooding in Pennsylvania from Tropical Storm Lee in 2011, the librarian at Middletown Public Library kept her patrons abreast of closing information on Facebook and Twitter. After the flooding, the library's website contained information about where residents could obtain recovery information. Farther up the Susquehanna River the West Pittston Public Library sustained major damage. Library staff used Facebook to post pictures and ask for volunteer help. In both cases, social media were incorporated to both inform and establish a virtual connection with patrons. Every library should have procedures in place for the following communication tools:

- Voice messaging
- Chat
- Twitter
- Facebook
- Website

FIGURE 4.1 Front Side of SCPReP

[Name of Library/Institution]

Pocket Response Plan (PReP)™

Revised [Date]

INSTITUTIONAL CONTACTS

[Examples of contact information needed—office or personnel names, phone numbers, e-mail addresses, etc.]

- Medical Center
- Office of Risk Management
- Emergency Command Center
- Health System Media Office
- Finance & Administration
- Dean of Medical School
- Student Affairs (Medical)
- Dean of the Nursing School
- Student Affairs (Nursing/Undergrad)
- Student Affairs (Nursing/Grad)
- Hospital Security
- Facilities Management
- Environmental Health & Safety
- Housekeeping
- Systems Control

LIBRARY DISASTER TEAM

[Examples of library disaster team and assignment of responsibilities]

Library Director
(coordinates decision making, liaison to outside sources)

Associate Director, Collection Management/Access Services
(Emergency Response Coordinator, liaison to the Assistant Director of Historical Collections, NN/LM, and backup libraries)

Associate Director, Information Services
(patron service recovery)

Associate Director, Library Technology & Development
(network environment, computer equipment and data)

Business Services Manager
(telephone service, facility, equipment and supplies, insurance)

Communications
(information updates to blogs and social sites)

Emergency Preparedness & Response Liaison
(EP&RP, documentation)

COMMUNICATION PLAN

[Sample]

Notification to the public and to staff

In an emergency that closes the library, the Library Disaster Team will contact service continuity personnel. Staff will be directed via e-mail or phone to call a designated library phone number for updated information.

Library's voicemail update

Patrons can call the Library Service Desk for information. To change the voicemail message, a designated person will call [phone number] and then enter the extension number for the Service Desk telephone. Use password [password]. The new message will give the current status and information about how to access the library's services and get help.

Social networking sites

A designated person will alert information to the library's homepage, blog site, Facebook page, and Twitter account. To update these sites, [insert procedures].

Communication with the media

The Library Director (or designee) is the only person who is authorized to speak with the media. Before releasing any information to the media, the [Media Office] must be contacted at [phone number].

SERVICE CONTINUITY PLAN

[Sample of explanation of services and how they will be maintained]

Online resources

Online resources are maintained at a vendor's remote location or on campus at [list server locations]. [Explain backup power situation]. After 3 to 5 days without power, core online resources such as UpToDate, MDConsult, R2, online journals, and StatRef [or other resources deemed "core"] might not be available at some locations. [Names of library staff] can field questions from patrons about individual title access problems.

Proxy

[Name] is responsible for proxy issues. [Name] is [his/her] backup.

Interlibrary loan

[Name, Title] can perform ILL functions from [his/her] home. In the event that [he/she] is not available to perform these functions, [explain backup arrangements, either within your library or with a partner library].

Library online chat and e-mail

Library staff will regularly check the IM chat site and the e-mail service maintained by [department or staff person's name]. [Manager's name] is responsible for coordinating this activity.

Library's webpage

The library's website is hosted by [name, location of server]. Use the library's homepage to announce disaster-related information. Updating the library's homepage relies on off-site Internet access and should only be activated by designated staff.

Access to library's print collection

If online access is not available, patient care personnel can access the library's print collection by contacting Security at [phone number]. All core textbooks and reference materials are located [specify].

SERVICE CONTINUITY TEAM

[List core services staff by name and title/function; sample following]

[Name], Library Director
Home: Cell:

[Name], Communications
Home: Cell:

[Name], Interlibrary Loan Operations
Home: Cell:

[Name], [Online Catalog] Operations
Home: Cell:

[Name], Service Desk Supervisor
Home: Cell:

[Name], Evening Supervisor
Home: Cell:

[Name], Information Services
Home: Cell:

[Name], Historical Collections
Home: Cell:

[Name], Collections
Home: Cell:

[Name], Administration
Home: Cell:

[Name], Webmaster
Home: Cell:

[Name], Head of Interlibrary Loan, [partner library]
Office:

[Name], IT
Home: Cell:

[Name], Databases
Home: Cell:

[Name], Collections, Emergency Response Coordinator
Home: Cell:

[Name], EP&RP Liaison
Home: Cell:

Source: Adapted from the PReP™ template courtesy of CoSA (Council of State Archivists), http://www.statearchivists.org/prepare/framework/prep.htm.

FIGURE 4.2 Back Side of SCPReP

[Name of Library/Institution]

Pocket Response Plan (PReP)™

Revised [Date]

PRIORITY LIST FOR COLLECTION RECOVERY
(See floor plans at right.)

High Priority
[Name of collection; e.g., Historical Collections]
(See priority list in third column.)

Medium Priority
Core Textbooks: On shelves [location(s) of shelving]
Reference Collection: On shelves [location(s) of shelving]
Journals, Core Titles: [location(s)]

Low Priority
Books: On shelves [location(s) of shelving]

VENDOR CONTACTS
[Name] (interlibrary loan): [phone number]
[Name] (journals): [phone number]
[Name] (book orders): [phone number]

[Databases]: [phone numbers]
[Others?]

FLOOR PLANS/LOCATIONS OF COLLECTIONS

[Insert labeled floor plan showing locations of high priority materials to be rescued.]

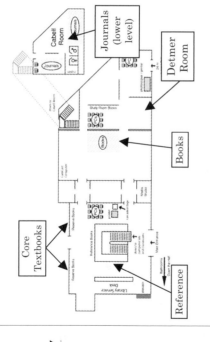

Core Textbooks

Cabell Room

Journals (lower level)

Detmer Room

Books

Reference

[Name of areas, floor shown, etc.]

HIGH PRIORITY RESCUE
ORDER LIST

[Specify highly valued materials and give locations and how they are to be accessed and rescued in an emergency. Paste in a floor plan of the area where these materials are located in the space to the left, and label the floor plan to show where the materials are, using names that correspond to your written instructions, such as room names, specific areas, etc.]

Supplies for collection salvage are located in the [location]. Additional supplies are in the [location].

GETTING HELP

NN/LM (National Network of Libraries of Medicine): (800) DEV-ROKS or (800) 338-7657 (business hours)

Contact [your NN/LM regional Network Coordinator] with regard to lending requests in DOCLINE, coordination of emergency response among members, resource sharing in emergency, and possible funding for replacement equipment.

NN/LM Emergency Preparedness & Response Toolkit: http://nnlm.gov/ep/

Local Preservation Librarian or Partner Conservator
[Name]
Office:
Cell:
Contact [Name] whenever print materials have been damaged.

[OCLC regional organization or other regional library network]: advice about saving collections, health and safety measures in an emergency, referrals to commercial salvage companies, etc. [Note whether on-site assistance is available.]

Northeast Document Conservation Center (NEDCC): (978) 470-1010 (24/7): will provide telephone advice to anyone about response to and recovery from a disaster that impacts library collections.

Salvage and Recovery Companies:
See the NN/LM Emergency Preparedness and Response Toolkit for links to commercial salvage companies

FIGURE 4.3 Mobile SCPReP

Photo by Daniel T. Wilson

FIGURE 4.4 SCPReP with Prepaid Phone Card

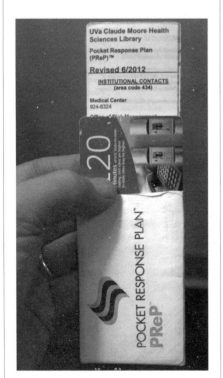

Photo by Daniel T. Wilson

Accompanying your SCPReP should be a prepaid phone card (see figure 4.4) that can be used at a pay phone or on a landline following a major disaster where cell phone calls are not getting through because of high volume. In most cases, text messages can get through, but if you need to talk to someone, a phone card and access to a landline will do the trick. Communication following a disaster is complex and is contingent on unstable and constantly changing variables. In September 2011, the Federal Communications System of FEMA released communication tips for use before, during, and after a disaster (see p. 55).

Video Calling

Use of a video calling system like FaceTime (http://www.apple.com/mac/facetime/?cid=oas-us-domains-facetime.com), Skype (http://www.skype.com/en/), or ooVoo (http://www.oovoo.com/) can enhance your ability to coordinate a response. These products are free and relatively easy to learn. Keep in mind, though, that the library-side client should be as portable as possible in order to show the actual incident, such as a burst pipe or flooding.

Video Conferencing

If your library is inhabitable and you need to meet regularly with your Service Continuity Team, consider subscribing to a video conferencing service. While video calling systems like those mentioned earlier can accommodate small groups, the image quality suffers when more participants are added. Therefore, if your contacts number six or more, investigate more robust video conferencing options, such as GoToMeeting (http://www.gotomeeting.com/) and WebEx (http://www.webex.com/). Prices of these services vary, but in return you'll get better transmission quality and reliability.

Column 4: Service Continuity Plan

Column 4, the Service Continuity Plan, is the heart of your plan because it contains the details for the continuation of core services. Although libraries will vary, staple core services usually include these two elements:

- Maintaining access to online resources through the library's website
- Providing online chat and e-mail to continue reference assistance and user support

In addition and, again, based on your users' needs, you may want to include a plan for interlibrary loan (borrowing only) and, finally, if your building space is needed, a plan for the continual provision of power and Internet. Key elements include clear instructions and redundancy to ensure continuation of services even when a primary person is not available. This is a very important part of planning because in a disaster or major service disruption it is unlikely that all members of the Service Continuity Team will be available to execute their roles.

Tips for Communicating Before, During, and After Disasters

When disaster strikes, you want to be able to communicate by both receiving and distributing information to others. You may need to call 9-1-1 for assistance, locate friends or family, or let loved ones know that you are okay. During disasters, communications networks could be damaged, lose power, or become congested. This fact sheet provides two important sets of tips. The first will help you prepare your home and mobile devices for a disaster. The second may help you communicate more effectively during and immediately after a disaster.

Before a Disaster: How to Prepare Your Home and Mobile Device

1. Maintain a list of emergency phone numbers in your cell phone and in or near your home phone.
2. Keep charged batteries and car-phone chargers available for backup power for your cell phone.
3. If you have a traditional landline (non-broadband or VOIP) phone, keep at least one non-cordless phone in your home because if it will work even if you lose power.
4. Prepare a family contact sheet. This should include at least one out-of-town contact that may be better able to reach family members in an emergency.
5. Program "In Case of Emergency" (ICE) contacts into your cell phone so emergency personnel can contact those people for you if you are unable to use your phone. Let your ICE contacts know that they are programmed into your phone and inform them of any medical issues or other special needs you may have.
6. If you are evacuated and have call-forwarding on your home phone, forward your home phone number to your cell phone number.
7. If you do not have a cell phone, keep a prepaid phone card to use if needed during or after a disaster.
8. Have a battery-powered radio or television available (with spare batteries).
9. Subscribe to text alert services from local or state governments to receive alerts in the event of a disaster. Parents should sign up for their school district emergency alert system.

During and After a Disaster: How to Reach Friends, Loved Ones, and Emergency Services

1. If you have a life-threatening emergency, call 9-1-1. Remember that you cannot currently text 9-1-1. If you are not experiencing an emergency, do not call 9-1-1. If your area offers 3-1-1 service or another information system, call that number for non-emergencies.
2. For non-emergency communications, use text messaging, e-mail, or social media instead of making voice calls on your cell phone to avoid tying up voice networks. Data-based services like texts and e-mails are less likely to experience network congestion. You can also use social media to post your status to let family and friends know you are okay. In addition to Facebook and Twitter, you can use resources such as the American Red Cross's Safe and Well program [http://safeandwell.communityos.org/cms/index.php].
3. Keep all phone calls brief. If you need to use a phone, try to convey only vital information to emergency personnel and/or family.
4. If you are unsuccessful in completing a call using your cell phone, wait ten seconds before redialing to help reduce network congestion.
5. Conserve your cell phone battery by reducing the brightness of your screen, placing your phone in airplane mode, and closing apps you are not using that draw power, unless you need to use the phone.
6. If you lose power, you can charge your cell phone in your car. Just be sure your car is in a well ventilated place (remove it from the garage) and do not go to your car until any danger has passed. You can also listen to your car radio for important news alerts.
7. Tune into broadcast television and radio for important news alerts. If applicable, be sure that you know how to activate the closed captioning or video description on your television.
8. If you do not have a hands-free device in your car, stop driving or pull over to the side of the road before making a call. Do not text on a cell phone, talk, or "tweet" without a hands-free device while driving.
9. Immediately following a disaster, resist using your mobile device to watch streaming videos, download music or videos, or play video games, all of which can add to network congestion. Limiting use of these services can help potentially life-saving emergency calls get through to 9-1-1.
10. Check www.ready.gov regularly to find other helpful tips for preparing for disasters and other emergencies.

Source: Reprinted from Federal Emergency Management Agency, 2011.

Column 5: Service Continuity Team

Let us rest for a moment and see what has been accomplished in this chapter. So far, you have listed your institutional/community contacts, provided contact information for each member of the disaster team, developed a communication plan, and detailed your SCP. In column 5, you will provide contact information and list the primary responsibility for each member of the SCT. Again, composition of this team will vary, but here are some suggested titles for team membership:

- Library Director
- Communication
- Interlibrary Loan
- Service Desk(s) Supervisor
- Reference Services
- Historical or Special Collections
- Collections Librarian
- Office Manager
- Web Administrator
- Head of Information Technology

Column 6: Priority Recovery List and Vendor Contacts

As you proceed to column 6, you are now on the back page of your plan, which focuses on collections and places to call if outside assistance is needed. Column 6 is divided into two sections: Priority List for Collection Recovery and Vendor Contacts.

Priority Recovery List

All libraries should have a prioritized collections recovery list for use in the event of a disaster that compromises collections, such as a flood, an earthquake, an explosion, or a tornado. Composing this list should not take much time at all, as your primary concern is for any unique or hard-to-replace items, followed by those items likely to be needed following a service disruption or disaster, and, finally, easily replaceable items. Here is a sample list for collection recovery:

- High priority: historical collections
- Medium priority: core textbooks, the reference collection, and the core journal collection
- Low priority: books in the general collection and non-core journal titles

Vendor List

The vendor list should include all vendors that need to be notified if the library is closed unexpectedly for three days or more. This list should include vendors for the interlibrary loan system, journals and books, major databases and online resources, and newspapers.

Column 7: Floor Plans

Floor plans might be needed in a disaster response, for instance, if the library is threatened or impacted by flooding or some kind of major water damage and, for the safety of library staff, no one other than first responders would be allowed in the building. Other scenarios might include an earthquake, tornado, or some kind of explosion that structurally damages the library to a degree that it is no longer safe to enter. In each of these cases, collections are at risk and need to be rescued, so floor plans should be clearly labeled indicating where the collections are located.

Column 8: High Priority Rescue Order List

When disaster strikes, think *people*, *collections*, and *services*, in that order. Protecting and rescuing unique or hard-to-replace materials therefore should come after saving people and before focusing on continuity of services. Use column 8 to prioritize all of these materials to a much higher degree of specificity than the list developed for column 6. Preferably, physically mark these items so that, if they do get damaged, any library staff member can manage the rescue process in the event that the curator is not available. Also specify what to do with damaged items, where to take them, and who to call. Here is how your rescue list might look:

- All items in the vault
- All items in the processing area
- The Richardson Collection found on the second shelving range
- All yearbooks
- All paintings and photographs

Column 9: Getting Help

Congratulations! You have made it to the final column, which contains contact information for those entities you will call on should you need outside assistance, whether for help continuing your services or rescuing your collections. Your SCPReP should contain contact information for the following:

- National Network of Libraries of Medicine (NN/LM): (800) DEV-ROKS or (800) 338-7657 during business hours, Monday through Friday.
- State library: This is particularly important for public libraries.
- Preservationist: A local preservationist can be a valuable asset who can provide preparedness advice as well as advice on recovering and preserving damaged materials.

- Library networks and conservation centers: Contact for advice about saving collections and referrals to commercial salvage companies. Some of these networks/centers provide these services toll-free, 24/7.
- Salvage and recovery company: Contact in the event that selected materials are damaged and freeze-drying is necessary. These companies also offer consultation services to help decide what materials should be saved and the process for that to happen.
- Backup library: A backup library can be an important tool in emergency response. In this column, list contact information for the library or libraries and the agreed-on backup arrangements. These services will vary from library to library but may contain the following:

  o Interlibrary loan
  o Chat/Ask a Librarian
  o Disaster response consultation

Conclusion

This chapter presented a fictional account of a disaster response that incorporated the one-page Service Continuity Pocket Response Plan, as well as a column-by-column guide on how to create a one-page Service Continuity Pocket Response Plan. Included were communication tips from FEMA for before, during, and after disasters, reinforcing the importance of a strong communication strategy throughout disaster planning, response, and recovery. The next chapter expands the discussion on mobility as well as social networking.

References

Council of State Archivists. 2011. "Pocket Response Plan (PReP)." Council of State Archivists. Last updated May 23. http://www.statearchivists.org/prepare/framework/prep.htm.

Federal Emergency Management Agency (FEMA). 2011. "How to Communicate During Disasters: Tip Sheet." FEMA. September 21. http://strathamnh.gov/Pages/StrathamNH_OEM/disastercommunicationtipsheet.pdf.

Tapping the Potential of Mobile Technologies and Social Media for Preparedness and Response

A visit to any public place, be it a library, shopping center, theater, or grocery store, provides ample evidence of the widespread use of smartphones and other mobile technologies. Accompanied by the exponential growth of social networking applications such as Facebook, Twitter, and YouTube, it is not surprising to observe the extent to which these devices and applications are so fully integrated into daily life. In addition to their high adoption rates, mobile technologies and social networking applications are fertile ground for organizations involved in disaster preparedness and response, as these entities recognize the importance of engaging current and potential volunteers, donors, and aid recipients in the virtual spaces they occupy. Because disasters often result in the displacement of people and contribute to dramatic interruptions in normal life, preparedness and response communities are integrating these technologies into their work flow to connect with the target groups they are trying to reach. It is important to consider that while the mobile environment is somewhat volatile it also provides new opportunities for connectivity and growth.

IN THIS CHAPTER:

✓ Mobile Technologies
✓ Social Networking
✓ Other Tools
✓ Challenges
✓ Conclusion
✓ References

Mobile Technologies

Although the mobile technology market includes a variety of devices, smartphones such as the iPhone and those operating on the Android platform are the most widespread. Research conducted by the Pew Research Center's Internet and American Life Project reflects that 55 percent of all adults in the United States own smartphones. Among these individuals, 34 percent use their phone for the majority of the searching and browsing they do online. Survey results also indicate that the reliance on smartphones for Internet access is high among groups, including Black and Latino users as well as those with little or no college education, with historically low rates of access to other computing devices (Duggan and Smith, 2013).

Active Shooter Incident at Virginia Tech

Following a tragic event attentions are often refocused on ways to improve preparedness and response efforts. The events that unfolded at Virginia Tech on April 16, 2007, when a student killed 32 fellow students and faculty and wounded many others before turning the gun on himself, highlighted the need for campus-wide alerting systems that can be deployed quickly to reach everyone in a targeted area or group. A review panel appointed by Virginia's then-governor Timothy Kaine issued an addendum to its initial report on the Virginia Tech tragedy in November 2009 (TriData Division, 2009). Although a campus alerting system was in place at the time of the shootings, the report indicates that several issues interfered with the timely implementation and use of that system. As a result of the events at Virginia Tech a number of institutions in both K-12 and higher education reviewed their policies and procedures for communicating with large constituencies. Many schools, colleges, and universities implemented or expanded their alerting systems and continue to test them regularly through drills or by using them to disseminate less urgent information. Such testing ensures that any problems can be worked out before the system is needed for an emergency or crisis situation. As is the case with Virginia Tech, systems typically employ voice-mail, text, and e-mail alerts and may also include audible warning systems such as sirens.

These statistics reflect that more people have access to devices that are not limited to a particular physical space and that enhance the users' ability to communicate and receive information. By capitalizing on these technologies, the disaster preparedness and response communities can maximize their ability to coordinate and communicate with volunteers and employees in the field as well as with those in need of assistance or information.

The availability and use of mobile technologies supports the integration of a "whole-community" approach to preparedness and response, an idea that the Federal Emergency Management Agency (FEMA) and others support. History reflects that in emergency situations ordinary people find themselves in the first responder role, which means, particularly early in a disaster, that they may be the individuals responsible for disseminating information about an event and providing assistance to those with immediate needs. According to FEMA Administrator W. Craig Fugate, adopting a whole-community approach is vital for a successful preparedness and response effort. "We need to move away from the mindset that Federal and State governments are always in the lead, and build upon the strengths of our local communities and, more importantly, our citizens. We must treat individuals and communities as key assets rather than liabilities" (Pisano-Pedigo, 2011: 6). The availability and widespread use of mobile technologies at all levels within a community assists with the transformation to a whole-community approach in the sense that a majority of citizens now have many means to connect with one another and become actively involved in the preparedness and response efforts where they are needed most.

Texting

Text messaging or SMS (short message service) is a communication method that allows users to send text between cell phones. According to data collected by the Pew Research Center on the use of mobile devices by adults, 81 percent of cell phone owners surveyed used their device to send or receive text messages (Duggan, 2013). Following the Emergency Social Data Summit organized by the American Red Cross in August 2010, it was reported that attendees considered texting to be the communications technology of choice because of its widespread use and availability as well as the likelihood that a brief text message would get through if networks are overloaded in the aftermath of a disaster (Harman and Huang, 2010). While these figures reflect that a majority of people are comfortable with texting, the preparedness and response community has incorporated ways to make it even easier to employ this technology in the event of an emergency.

In addition to using mobile devices and technologies to transfer information both from and to affected populations, there is also increased scrutiny being applied to the analysis of mobile phone network usage data in order to follow populations in crises. In a study examining the movement of individuals following the earthquake in Haiti based on mobile phone data, Bengtsson and colleagues (2011) found that there is tremendous potential for rapidly targeting relief efforts in areas with prevalent mobile phone use.

Preliminary research suggests that it is feasible to use network usage data to locate areas with large numbers of people in need (Bengtsson et al., 2011).

Apps

Mobile technologies like smartphones offer users an endless variety of apps that allow them to customize and tailor the information and services available at their fingertips. Apps relevant to emergency preparedness and response efforts include those targeting particular types of events, such as hurricanes; those which facilitate communication with family, friends, and first responders; and those which provide assistance with first aid and disaster planning. Some of the more popular apps relevant to preparedness and response include those focused on communication (Twitter, Facebook); disaster planning (Disaster Caster, Emergency Preparedness Checklist); GPS/location-based functionality (Here I Am, Life360, Emergency Distress Beacon); radio/scanners/weather info (Emergency Radio, Weather Alert, EZ Radar); first aid/survival (Pocket First Aid and CPR Guide, iSurvive Wilderness Support); and information for first responders (REMM, WISER). Also worth mentioning are relevant mobile-optimized websites such as MedlinePlus Mobile and PubMed Mobile from the National Library of Medicine. A detailed list of apps available for smartphones and other mobile devices is provided in the appendix. To successfully deploy and utilize these apps, it is important for both responders and the public to investigate and experiment before disaster strikes, and according to data collected by the American Red Cross, 20 percent of the public are doing just that. Among survey respondents the most popular types of emergency apps included those providing weather forecasts, first aid information, and disaster preparedness tips (American Red Cross, 2012).

Social Networking

When it comes to connecting online, users have a number of options. Many users will participate in more than one community or network, depending on their specific information needs and whom they are seeking to connect with. Likewise, organizations involved in preparedness and response activities are becoming more aware of the benefits of social media and are participating in a variety of online communities to "listen" and gather information as well as using the channels to distribute their organizational message and push relevant content to users. In many ways, social networking facilitates the dissemination of information because everyone in the community can assist with getting the word out, even to the point that the message may go "viral." Organizations that monitor posts and comments contributed by socially networked users are better equipped to tailor their message to the communities they serve. Participation in social networking communities by responders and community members helps ensure that the information and service needs unique to a particular disaster or emergency are "heard," increasing

CDC PSAs

Prepared text messages designed for mobile devices are available through the Centers for Disease Control Emergency Preparedness and Response website. These mini public service announcements (PSAs) are geared toward keeping people safe following a natural disaster or emergency situation and include avoiding carbon monoxide poisoning during power outages, driving through high water, determining if prescription drugs are safe to use, and maintaining building safety. A complete list is available at http://www.bt.cdc.gov/disasters/psa/textmessages.asp.

App to the Rescue

Dan Woolley, an aid worker in Haiti at the time of the 2010 earthquake, credits Pocket First Aid and CPR from Jive Media with saving his life. While trapped in the rubble of a collapsed hotel in Port-au-Prince, Woolley used the instructions provided by the app to treat his wounds and manage his situation until rescue workers found him more than 60 hours after the quake.

(Levs, 2010)

National Weather Service Posting Information

The National Weather Service, which has more than 218,000 "likes," uses Facebook as a supplemental channel for improving weather awareness. Postings to the Facebook page highlight activities of interest and importance to both the weather community and the public, and they include NWS meetings, constituent and partner engagement activities, and public education efforts. Questions or comments about local forecasts or local advisories/watches/warnings need to be submitted to the issuing local Weather Forecast Offices. The local Weather Forecast Offices are listed at http://www.weather.gov/organization.php.

the likelihood that those needs can be addressed. Many preparedness and response professionals emphasize that all response is local—active participation in social media helps everyone involved in the response meet that goal. It is important to note that local agencies and television and radio stations have embraced social networking outlets just as readily as their regional and national counterparts. Many of these entities have presences on Facebook and Twitter and have developed their own specialized apps for providing weather alerts, emergency information, and other news to their constituencies.

There are a number of social networking platforms, and as with most technology, new applications are continually introduced. Those highlighted in this chapter were chosen because they have a significant user base and have been utilized by the preparedness and response communities.

Facebook

Facebook provides an excellent illustration of the symbiotic relationship between mobile technologies and social networking. From its launch in February 2004, the Facebook community has grown to over one billion active users today. With the introduction of Facebook Mobile in April 2006, statistics now reflect that 945 million users access the community through mobile devices, and these users are more active than those users who visit the community through other means ("Facebook Key Facts," 2014). In a survey conducted by the American Red Cross, over 58 percent of respondents were Facebook users compared to YouTube's distant second at 31 percent. Perhaps even more significant, survey results indicated that 14 percent have used Facebook to obtain information about a disaster or emergency situation, 75 percent have provided information about emergencies or "newsworthy events" via their Facebook pages, and 86 percent would use Facebook to update friends and family about their safety in an emergency (American Red Cross, 2010).

Individuals are using Facebook to share real-time information with friends and family as well as to reconnect with individuals when relationships have been interrupted. Facebook can facilitate sharing information about emergencies, initiate responses to calls for help or assistance, provide aid in locating people who are missing, and determine if friends and family are safe. Many agencies and organizations are also utilizing the vast Facebook network to provide information about themselves, including photos, videos, and events. The organizations and the visitors to their pages can monitor an ongoing dialogue through visitor comments and those indicating they "like" a particular post.

YouTube

Launched officially in December 2005, YouTube's video-sharing platform now supports monthly views of over six billion hours of video, with more than 100 hours of video being uploaded every minute. More than one billion unique users visit YouTube every month ("YouTube Statistics," 2014). Users can search or browse for videos, upload their own creations, and establish their own YouTube channel by setting up a free account. The mobile version of YouTube allows users to record and upload videos directly from their phones in addition to the search and commenting features provided in the standard environment.

Eyewitness accounts of natural disasters and other emergency situations are easily found on YouTube, with the more dramatic videos, such as those captured during the 2011 Japan earthquake/tsunami and Hurricane Sandy in 2012, having billions of views. For organizations and agencies involved in preparedness and response YouTube also provides a free, accessible platform to disseminate timely and accurate safety information, how-to videos, and other content.

Twitter

As the most popular microblogging application, Twitter is all about information exchange, allowing users to follow conversation streams that they find interesting. Users can also contribute to these online conversations through tweets, with each tweet consisting of 140 or fewer characters. Finding updates or tweets about a particular event or those generated by a specific organization is easier through the use of "hashtags." Hashtags are created by placing a pound sign (#) in front of a word in your tweet. The hashtag then becomes a link that allows anyone reading that tweet to easily find all of the other tweets that include the same hashtag. In addition, hashtags can be used as search terms.

There are also a number of applications that allow users to customize their Twitter experience. Mobile.twitter.com allows users to experience Twitter on any mobile device. Although Tweetdeck began as a third-party application, it has been acquired by Twitter and offers users the ability to coordinate updates for a number of social networking interfaces, including Twitter, Facebook, LinkedIn, and Foursquare, as well as flexible organization options. Twitpic makes it easy for users to share real-time photos and videos via Twitter by posting through a mobile device, the Twitpic site, or e-mail.

In the context of disaster preparedness and response, Twitter may be the most heavily used social networking tool because it gives users the ability to immediately transmit pictures and text from the scene as well as provide real-time updates about locations to avoid, where to obtain services, and how to donate money or supplies.

Other Tools

A number of tools are emerging that facilitate the transformation of raw data, through crisis mapping and other techniques, into actionable information for individuals responding to an emergency. While being able to identify trends from user-generated data holds a great deal of promise for

Hurricane Preparedness on YouTube

The National Hurricane Center has produced a series of YouTube videos for National Hurricane Preparedness Week. The series of seven public service announcements includes a historical overview of hurricane activity; reviews of hurricane hazards such as storm surges, winds, and flooding; and the importance of a preparedness plan and safety tips. In addition to being available on YouTube, links to the videos and other hurricane preparedness information are highlighted on the Center's website at http://www.nhc.noaa.gov/prepare/.

Crisis Information on Twitter

The crash of U.S. Airways Flight 1549 into the freezing waters of New York's Hudson River near midtown Manhattan on January 15, 2009, illustrates how Twitter can be utilized in a crisis. Minutes following the crash, Twitter user Janis Krums, who was on a passenger ferry near the crash site, took a photo of the downed plane and posted it to Twitpic. Krums tweeted, "There's a plane in the Hudson. I'm on the ferry going to pick up the people. Crazy." Thousands of people viewed the photo and created links to the image while many others responded to his tweet by posting comments via Twitter. Krums was in an ideal position and equipped with the tools and expertise necessary to begin the flow of information about this disaster immediately. Thanks to the quick instincts of the pilot and crew as well as the rapid coordination of rescue efforts, injuries were minimized and no lives were lost.

(Johnston and Marrone, 2009)

the public health, preparedness, and response communities, it is important to note that a 2012 survey of state, county, and local emergency personnel reflected that many remain unfamiliar with these types of resources (Su, Wardell, and Thorkildsen, 2013).

Google Trends/Google Flu Trends

Google Trends examines a subset of searches to determine how many searches have been conducted for the terms entered in relation to the total number of Google searches done over time. Graphical representations of the search volume are then displayed along with a graph that shows the number of times the terms were included in Google News stories. When Google Trends detects an increase in the number of news stories that contain the search term(s) the headline of a story is displayed. An interesting public health application of Google Trends is illustrated by Google Flu Trends (2014). By analyzing search terms entered by users that were related to influenza and then comparing these query counts with surveillance data collected by the Centers for Disease Control and Prevention, researchers discovered that search queries were good predictors of when and where flu was present (Ginsberg et al., 2009). While more research needs to be conducted, analyzing user-generated data may enhance the predictive capability of responses to pandemics and crises and provide valuable lead time for responders.

Ushahidi

Ushahidi, a Swahili word meaning witness or testimony, is a free, open source platform that was created initially following post-election violence in Kenya early in 2008. Ushahidi now has a growing community of developers who are expanding and tailoring its functionality to a variety of applications and uses. Ushahidi's basic tenets are that the platform is easy to use, accessible to anyone, and deployable worldwide. Information can be gathered from any digital device and submitted in the form of a text message, videos or photos, or more lengthy reports. Once the information is submitted it is displayed in almost real time on an interactive map. "The Ushahidi engine is there for 'everyday' people to let the world know what is happening in their area during a crisis, emergency, or other situation. Bringing awareness, linking those in need to those who can assist, and providing the framework for better visualization of information graphically" ("Ushahidi 1-Pager," 2014: 2).

Crowdmap is a hosted system that allows anyone to implement Ushahidi without having to install the platform on his or her own web server. A third extension of Ushahidi is SwiftRiver, a free, open source platform designed to help anyone manage the huge amount of information that is generated through multiple data streams in the immediate aftermath of a crisis or disaster. SwiftRiver facilitates the ability to categorize, filter, and verify

Storm Damage Displayed with Crowdmap

Crowdmap was deployed in Vermont to document the extensive flooding following Hurricane Irene in August 2011. Specific instructions are available on the main page (http://vtirene.crowdmap.com/) to encourage everyone to report damage from the storm. The site also encourages those providing aid to post information about where assistance can be obtained and those in need can request help. All information can be displayed graphically on a map, and the site also allows users to browse a chronological list of incidents in addition to information from official organizations and news agencies.

information from a variety of sources, including Twitter, text messages, and e-mail ("The SwiftRiver Platform," 2014).

Foursquare

Foursquare is one example of a location-based service that utilizes the global positioning system (GPS) functionality of smartphones. Users can easily share their location and information about their current surroundings with friends through an app or text messaging. Current figures reflect that Foursquare has over 45 million users around the world and that these users are "checking in" more than 5 billion times per day ("About Foursquare," 2014). Businesses are also using tools like Foursquare to reach existing and potential customers; their practices could be adopted by preparedness and response organizations to deliver and collect crucial information before, during, and after a crisis. The utilization of location-based services in times of crisis or following a disaster could facilitate the mobilization of volunteers and supplies, guide responders to problem areas or to people in need of assistance or rescue, and provide real-time, on-the-ground information to other people in the affected geographic area.

Challenges

While the benefits are many, incorporating social networking into a unified response is not without its challenges. In an article published in the *New England Journal of Medicine*, Merchant, Elmer, and Lurie (2011) provide a concise overview of issues that the preparedness and response community need to keep in mind with regard to the implementation and integration of social media data and mobile technologies. While it is evident that use of these devices and services is growing at an exponential rate, there still may be areas where access is limited and with populations that could also be classified as high risk and in need of services.

Authenticating information from unofficial channels such as Twitter or Facebook is a concern as well. How does an agency confirm that information shared by the public is correct? Identifying effective and efficient ways to filter the flood of information and isolating those pieces which are actionable is a genuine cause for concern. Privacy and confidentiality also have to be considered when monitoring social media outlets and then potentially sharing the information with a broader audience. As Maron noted in a 2013 article published in *Scientific American*, Hurricane Sandy provided a real-world laboratory to examine the flow of inaccurate information through social media channels following a disaster. In an attempt to mitigate the effect of any misinformation, FEMA established Rumor Control (http://m.fema.gov/sandy-rumor-control) following Sandy and has since used the tool in other disasters.

Industry Responses to Mobile Infrastructure Challenges

Questions surrounding the adequacy of the mobile network infrastructure during a crisis are certainly valid. Being able to fully utilize these tools in the periods of extreme usage often seen in disasters is critical. Industry is responding to these concerns in a variety of ways. For example, Verizon has developed a high-tech menagerie, namely GOATs, COWs, and COLTs, to bolster the essential infrastructure in high-demand situations. A GOAT, or Generator On A Trailer, is employed in power outages or when the existing power supply is inadequate. A COW, or Cell On Wheels, enables the company to boost cell phone coverage temporarily in an area where many customers are congregating, as they might in the event of a disaster. Similar to the COW, a COLT, or Cell On a Light Truck, provides or expands network coverage quickly and is ideal for remote or rural areas.

(Miller, 2011)

Another approach to address the overwhelming flood of data produced by an emergency situation is to utilize Virtual Operations Support Teams (VOSTs). Each team is typically composed of both emergency management professionals and volunteers who provide data curation and analysis services to colleagues responding in the field. If multiple VOSTs are involved in a response, a Virtual Operations Support Group (VOSG) may be established to coordinate the efforts of the various VOSTs (Reuter, 2012). Blum and colleagues (2013) illustrate how VOSTs can be incorporated into emergency response efforts and highlight specific roles these individuals can play.

Rigorous research is needed to evaluate the use and effectiveness of utilizing social networking and mobile technologies in preparedness and response activities. Outcomes data is essential to identify those technologies which provide an adequate return on investment and positively impact preparedness and response efforts (Merchant, Elmer, and Lurie, 2011). Developing a system to cumulate the flood of information, document the lessons learned while the event is ongoing, and synthesize the information so that assistance can be dispatched is critical as well.

Finally, a huge challenge is the dynamic nature of mobile technologies and social media. Organizations and individuals alike struggle with how to keep up, realizing that the hot new app or platform today may disappear without a trace tomorrow. How should the preparedness and response community utilize and manage the tools currently in use but still keep their eyes on the horizon and be ready to adapt to changing technologies? How can libraries assist both users and responders with these needs? While these are not easy questions to grapple with, it is clear that waiting for a single standard or the "perfect" tool is not an option. Individuals and agencies must acquaint themselves with the possibilities and begin to experiment with and use these tools so that when a crisis occurs the learning curve is small and the appropriate technologies can be implemented quickly.

Conclusion

Because mobile technologies and social media are now embedded in the everyday routines of millions, the integration of these tools into preparedness, response, and recovery activities will continue. Evidence already exists illustrating that ordinary citizens are better equipped to engage at all levels of the process and that professionals are utilizing these tools to connect with more people, deliver more services, and disseminate more accurate information quickly and efficiently in times of crisis. The use of mobile technologies and social media fosters an environment where the whole-community approach to preparedness and response can flourish. Individuals from all walks of life can participate and contribute to finding and delivering solutions to problems, and participation at some level by more people is certainly a reasonable expectation with the proliferation of these tools. By leveling the playing field, many now have a place at the table and, as a result, responsibility is distributed and shared. While some hurdles exist with the implementation and integration of these tools, the benefits seem to outweigh the risks. Experience has shown that communities are stronger when they stand together in the face of adversity, and mobile technologies and social media tools excel at bringing people together.

References

"About Foursquare." 2014. Foursquare. https://foursquare.com/about.

American Red Cross. 2010. "Social Media in Disasters and Emergencies." American Red Cross. http://www.redcross.org/www-files/ Documents/pdf/other/SocialMediaSlideDeck.pdf.

———. 2012. "More Americans Using Mobile Apps in Emergencies." American Red Cross. http://www.redcross.org/news/press-release/ More-Americans-Using-Mobile-Apps-in-Emergencies.

Bengtsson, L., X. Lu, A. Thorson, R. Garfield, and J. von Schreeb. 2011. "Improved Response to Disasters and Outbreaks by Tracking Population Movements with Mobile Phone Network Data: A Post-Earthquake Geospatial Study in Haiti." *PLoS Medicine* 8, no. 8 (August): e1001083. doi:10.1371/journal.pmed.1001083.

Blum, J. R., A. Eichhorn, S. Smith, M. Sterle-Contala, and J. R. Cooperstock. 2013. "Real-Time Emergency Response: Improved Management of Real-Time Information during Crisis Situations." *Journal of Multimodal User Interfaces* (December). doi:10.1007/ s12193-013-0139-7.

Duggan, M. 2013. "Cell Phone Activities 2013." Pew Research Internet Project. September 19. http://www.pewinternet.org/2013/09/19/ cell-phone-activities-2013/.

Duggan, M., and A. Smith. 2013. "Cell Internet Use 2013." Pew Research Internet Project. September 16. http://www.pewinternet .org/2013/09/16/cell-internet-use-2013/.

"Facebook Key Facts." 2014. Facebook. https://newsroom.fb.com/ Key-Facts.

Ginsberg, J., M. H. Mohebbi, R. S. Patel, L. Brammer, M. S. Smolinski, and L. Brilliant. 2009. "Detecting Influenza Epidemics Using Search Engine Query Data." *Nature* 457, no. 7232 (February 19): 1012–1014.

Google Flu Trends. 2014. Google. http://www.google.org/flutrends/.

Harman, Wendy, and Gloria Huang. 2010. "The Path Forward: American Red Cross Crisis Data Summit Wrap-Up." Scribd. http://www.scribd .com/doc/40080608/The-Path-Forward-ARC-Crisis-Data-Summit-Wrap-Up.

Johnston, Lauren, and Matt Marrone. 2009. "Twitter User Becomes Star in US Airways Crash—Janis Krums Sets Internet Abuzz with iPhone Photo." *Daily News,* January 16. http://www.nydailynews.com/new-york/twitter-user-star-airways-crash-janis-krums-sets-internet-abuzz-iphone-photo-article-1.408174.

Levs, Josh. 2010. "Trapped Father Survives with Help of Phone App." *CNN,* January 24. http://www.cnn.com/2010/WORLD/americas/01/24/haiti.survivor.phone.app/index.html?_s=PM:WORLD.

Maron, Dina Fine. 2013. "How Social Media Is Changing Disaster Response." *Scientific American*, June 7. http://www.scientificamerican.com/article/how-social-media-is-changing-disaster-response/.

Merchant, R. M., S. Elmer, and N. Lurie. 2011. "Integrating Social Media into Emergency-Preparedness Efforts." *New England Journal of Medicine* 365, no. 4 (July 28): 289–291.

Miller, Michael J. 2011. "How Verizon Tests and Delivers Wireless Coverage: Photos." *Forward Thinking* (blog), March 24. http://forwardthinking.pcmag.com/phones/282341-how-verizon-tests-and-delivers-wireless-coverage-photos.

Pisano-Pedigo, Lynn. 2011. "Whole Community of Emergency Management." *Partners in Preparedness*, March. http://www.fema.gov/pdf/about/regions/regionviii/risc_0311.pdf.

Reuter, S. 2012. "What Is a Virtual Operations Support Team?" *idisaster 2.0* (blog), February 15. http://idisaster.wordpress.com/2012/02/13/what-is-a-virtual-operations-support-team/.

Su, Y. S., C. Wardell, and Z. Thorkildsen. 2013. "Social Media in the Emergency Management Field: 2012 Survey Results." CNA Corporation. June 3. http://www.cna.org/research/2013/social-media-emergency-management-field.

"The SwiftRiver Platform." 2014. Ushahidi. http://www.ushahidi.com/products/swiftriver-platform.

TriData Division, System Planning Corporation. 2009. "Mass Shootings at Virginia Tech: Addendum to the Report of the Review Panel." Virginia Tech Digital Library and Archives. http://scholar.lib.vt.edu/prevail/docs/April16ReportRev20091204.pdf.

"Ushahidi 1-Pager." 2014. Ushahidi. http://www.ushahidi.com/-/docs/Ushahidi_1-Pager.pdf.

"YouTube Statistics." 2014. YouTube. http://www.youtube.com/yt/press/statistics.html.

Personal Preparedness and Possible Impact on Library Services

When a disaster strikes "all hands are needed on deck," but unfortunately this possibility is often the exception rather than the rule. If the disaster is widespread, many employees, including key members of the disaster recovery team, might be unavailable because of mandatory evacuation, personal property loss, depression or anxiety, personal injury, or lack of child care, basic utilities, and transportation. One way to alleviate the possibility of extended absences is to ensure that all staff members have a personal preparedness plan for home and family. Planning ahead can help to mitigate the effects of a disaster in many ways, including saving lives, protecting property, ensuring a speedier recovery, and supporting good mental health. Many national, regional, and local agencies have valuable resources to assist in personal preparedness, and these resources are often focused on the areas listed earlier. Disasters can be personally devastating and can keep valuable staff out of the library for long periods of time; as a result, every library's COOP plan should include a section on personal preparedness to decrease the possibility that important staff members will be unavailable during a crisis. This chapter begins by outlining the basic steps for individual preparedness and response and then introduces a variety of potential threats and library stories relevant to those threats.

IN THIS CHAPTER:

✓ Create a Kit

✓ Make a Plan

✓ Specific Threats

✓ Conclusion

✓ References

Create a Kit

Most national agencies that deal with disasters and disaster planning recommend having on hand a basic emergency supply kit. Every household should contain adequate supplies to ensure that occupants can survive without assistance for some period of time. According to Ready America, the American Red Cross, and other reputable agencies, a basic kit should include the items discussed in this section.

Personal Preparedness Resources
- *American Red Cross* http://www.redcross.org/
- *2-1-1* http://211.org/
- *DisasterAssistance.gov* http://www.disasterassistance.gov/
- *Emergency Preparedness and Response (CDC)* http://www.bt.cdc.gov/
- *MedlinePlus* http://www.nlm.nih.gov/medlineplus/
- *National Weather Service* http://weather.gov/
- *Ready.gov* http://www.ready.gov/

Water

At minimum, store a three-day supply of water per person based on at least one gallon of water per person per day for drinking, cooking, and sanitation. Children, nursing mothers, residents in warm climates, and people who are ill may need more water. Water should be stored in tightly sealed plastic containers. Prior to a disaster people will often fill bathtubs with water to be used for sanitation purposes.

Food

At all times maintain a three-day supply of nonperishable foods that require no refrigeration or preparation and very little water. Choose items that all household members, especially children, will eat. Good foods to have on hand include:

- Ready-to-eat canned meats
- Fruits and vegetables
- Protein or fruit bars
- Dry cereal or granola
- Peanut butter
- Dried fruit
- Nuts
- Crackers
- Canned juices
- Nonperishable pasteurized milk
- High-energy foods
- Comfort/stress foods

Loss of power can be caused by a variety of events and can take several days to restore. Keep in mind that without electricity or a sustainable cold source, refrigerated or frozen food can quickly become unsafe. Storing adequate quantities of nonperishable food items will ensure that everyone in the household receives the proper nutrition. Remember to include a manual can opener and eating utensils.

First Aid Supplies

Cuts, burns, and other minor injuries are common in emergency situations so having basic supplies readily available is a good idea. Be sure to check the expiration dates on perishable items and replace as necessary. First aid kits should contain the following:

- Latex and/or sterile gloves
- Sterile dressings
- Cleansing agents such as antibiotic towelettes
- Antibiotic ointment
- Burn ointment
- Adhesive bandages
- Eye-wash solution
- Thermometer

Medications

A seven-day supply of any prescription medications should also be included in an emergency supply kit. Because some medications, such as insulin, need to be kept at a cool temperature, a cooler with ice or dry ice may be required. Additionally, nonprescription medications such as pain relievers, antidiarrheal agents, antacids, and laxatives are important components to include. Other supplies such as scissors, tweezers, and petroleum jelly can be useful. Depending on the specific needs of individuals in the household, there may be other necessities such as denture supplies, contact lens solution, or a spare pair of eye glasses. Finally, include medical supplies such as glucose and blood pressure monitoring equipment.

Nose, Mouth, and Skin Protection

Air pollutants, such as the development of mold, which frequently accompanies flooding, can severely compromise air quality following a disaster. For this reason it is advisable to keep face masks constructed of densely woven material on hand. Other materials such as heavy-weight plastic garbage bags or plastic sheeting can be used to protect the skin. Duct tape and scissors might be needed to shape the materials to fit. These materials can also be used to block windows, doors, and air vents if the crisis requires occupants to "shelter in place." Work/plastic gloves will provide some protection to hands while cleaning up debris in and around damaged areas.

Infant Supplies

Young children have special needs so consider adding the following supplies when appropriate:

- Formula and/or powdered milk
- Diapers

- Bottles
- Medications
- Moist towelettes
- Diaper rash ointment

Electronics Equipment and Accessories

In this age most individuals consider cell phones to be a necessity even under normal conditions. In times of disaster, cell phones provide vital communication links, with the ability to send text messages when cell towers fail. But, a cell phone is only valuable if it is charged. The caveat is that some cars will charge a phone even if not turned on and some will not, and a shortage of gasoline can negate the positive effect of having a vehicle adapter. Because power outages are common in a disaster, explore options for charging cell phones and other devices when there is no electricity and include any necessary equipment in the emergency supply kit. A high-speed Internet broadband card can also assist the flow of communication, particularly when individuals are geographically displaced because of the event. Battery powered or hand-cranked weather radios and AM/FM radios can relay valuable information about current conditions and events. Keep spare batteries on hand to maintain the connections.

Written Documents

Many important documents should be accessible following a disaster:

- Medication lists and pertinent medical records
- Proof of address
- Deed or lease to home or apartment
- Passports
- Birth certificates
- Insurance policies
- Family and emergency contact information
- Extra cash
- Credit cards with available balances
- Maps of the area

It is advisable to keep all of these items in a portable locked box so they can be easily located and transported in the event of an evacuation. Copies may also be scanned and stored digitally.

Special Needs

Meeting the needs of individuals who are elderly, physically/mentally disabled, or suffering from acute or chronic health conditions requires extra planning. Contact local authorities in advance if the person will need special assistance in an evacuation. Nationally, the United Way supports a 211 phone hotline that provides preregistration for evacuation assistance. The

Red Cross also suggests that, in addition to the planning outlined in this chapter, people with special needs should have a personal support network that can help them prepare for and respond to a disaster. A personal assessment, prepared in advance, of tasks that will be handled independently along with tasks requiring assistance is particularly important to have on hand for anyone with special needs.

Pet Supplies

Pets are an important part of many households, so their needs should be considered as well. Be sure to pack appropriate equipment (carrier, collar, leash, bowls, etc.), documents (registration/license, medical records), and any medications, as well as food and water.

Other Items

The list could go on and on, but additional items useful in most kits include flashlights, lanterns, and/or candles; two-way radios; an extra set of house and car keys; whistle; matches; rain gear; extra clothing, hats, and sturdy shoes; duct tape; liquid household bleach; entertainment items; and blankets or sleeping bags.

Make a Plan

The risk of a major disaster in any geographic area can be estimated using the risk assessment methods introduced in chapter 1. Always keep in mind, however, that a disaster can occur anytime and anyplace. For example, in the spring of 2011 unusual tornadoes struck both Minneapolis, Minnesota, and Springfield, Massachusetts, causing widespread damage and injuries. Because it is very likely that all family members will not be together when a disaster strikes, it is important to plan in advance how everyone will contact one another as well as designating a few potential locations for reuniting. The following steps will help.

Communications

Identify an out-of-town family member or friend as the primary contact person. Often following a disaster it is easier to place a long-distance call than to call across town, so this individual might be in a better position to facilitate communication and provide status updates. Be sure that every family member has an up-to-date phone list and is equipped with a cell phone.

Add important emergency numbers to the list of contacts in all phones and group these individuals under ICE (In Case of Emergency). Emergency personnel will often check ICE listings in crises to connect with emergency contacts. Make sure family and/or friends are aware they are listed as ICE contacts. Because text messages are often transmitted during network

DHS and HHS Can Further Strengthen Coordination for Chemical, Biological, Radiological, and Nuclear Risk Assessments

The anthrax attacks of 2001 and more recent national reports have raised concerns that the United States is vulnerable to attacks with chemical, biological, radiological, and nuclear (CBRN) agents. Because of the potential consequences of such attacks, members of Congress have expressed the need for the Departments of Homeland Security (DHS) and Health and Human Services (HHS) to coordinate in assessing risks posed by CBRN agents. GAO [Government Accountability Office] was asked to examine how DHS and HHS coordinate on the development of CBRN risk assessments and the extent to which they have institutionalized such efforts. GAO examined relevant laws, presidential directives, collaboration best practices, and internal control standards; analyzed DHS and HHS CBRN risk assessments; and interviewed DHS and HHS officials.

(Reprinted from U.S. Government Accountability Office, 2011)

disruptions when cell phone calls cannot be completed, make sure all family members are comfortable with text messaging. Be aware that, depending on individual contracts and providers, there may be additional charges to use text functions.

Subscribe to alert services provided by local communities, Community Emergency Response Teams, universities, school districts, and employers. These services automatically send an e-mail or a text and/or call subscribers to relay information about everything from weather alerts, road closures, and school closures to other local emergencies.

Deciding to Stay or Go

All household members should discuss the criteria that will help them decide whether to evacuate in the event of a disaster. If evacuation zones are prescribed for the entities responsible for managing a disaster, this decision will be easy. Either way, all family members should understand the plan for both scenarios. Local media such as television and radio, along with the subscribed alert services mentioned previously, can assist in making this important decision.

While there are many resources that can be used to help create a personal preparedness plan, one that is recommended is the Family Emergency Plan made available through the Ready America website at http://ready .adcouncil.org/fep/.

Specific Threats

So far, this chapter has emphasized the importance of personal preparedness to improve the likelihood that employees are safe and available if disaster strikes the library. Focus shifts now to an overview of specific threats and includes a number of lessons learned, shared by libraries that have responded to these threats.

Iowa Flooding

In June 2008 record flooding in Iowa caused billions of dollars in damage and impacted more than 300 communities. The Cedar River crested in Cedar Rapids at over 31 feet, nearly 20 feet above flood stage and 12 feet higher than the historic flood of 1993. Nine rivers in Iowa reached all-time record flood levels, and 85 of the state's 99 counties were declared disaster areas. Several major libraries and museums were affected, and a number of cultural institutions were devastated. Fortunately, training and long-established networks greatly enhanced our ability to respond to the unprecedented flooding.

The Main Library on the University of Iowa (UI) campus sits along the Iowa River and experienced minor flooding, although the library was still closed for several weeks to repair damage to equipment and the building. Thanks to quick action by library staff members prior to the flooding, employees and equipment were relocated before the flood and services resumed one week after the flood. Other campus libraries and buildings, as well as libraries and cultural institutions throughout the region, received major flood damage. The staff at the UI libraries learned valuable lessons from this experience.

Managing a Disaster

1. The ideal, of course, is to have an up-to-date disaster plan complete with a list of contacts and a disaster response company on contract ahead of time with at least some specifics worked out. At minimum, have a list of companies on hand.

2. Keep a log or journal during the response and recovery period. Record names and phone numbers of those involved, at least those involved in major decision making, and record decisions made.

3. An important part of a recovery process is careful planning. Planning can be done while waiting to be allowed back into the building or area. Staff needs to be in agreement as to who is in charge of what. Assignments can be made: Who will coordinate the overall response effort? Who will work with the media, volunteers, and the insurance company? Who will be responsible for what area or collection type? Storage for salvaged material will need to be located. Transportation for collections needs to be secured. Collection priorities need to be reviewed. Ideally, everyone will meet with the disaster response company in a sit-down meeting to introduce one another and review the overall strategy. It's very important that everyone is on the same page before beginning the recovery process. Participants will be stressed to the max, and the situation will keep changing. Having a common understanding of goals and directions will greatly assist during this very trying part of the recovery process.

4. Sharing, instead of competing for, resources will enhance a recovery process. When the disaster response team could not get into the National Czech and Slovak Museum and Library, they moved to the African American Museum of Iowa. The team worked to keep salvage operations going at both museums. Supplies were shared. Strategies learned at one site were used at the other. When members of the teams met with the disaster response company to coordinate the recovery efforts, the company not only agreed to work for both museums but offered to give a group discount. Later, they agreed to let us put out a call for other entities to share the freezer truck space.

5. A key piece of the planning process is identifying who has the power to get you into the disaster area and into a building.

6. At the very beginning of the process, advise staff that plans will constantly change and that many decisions will be made on the fly.

7. Follow all the disaster response steps—ensure the building is stable before entering; assess damage before going to work; establish salvage priorities; divide into teams; assign a coordinator; keep the disaster recovery service in the loop; assign one or more individuals to handle public relations, insurance agents, and volunteers; document conditions of the collections and building structure as best you can; and practice safety at all times.

8. Have the insurance agent, lawyer, board president, or whoever will be making money decisions on-site as soon as possible. If they can see the damage first hand, they'll be more inclined to help and more receptive when money requests come in. They'll be able to advise and assist with the steps you'll need to take to secure reimbursement.

Historic Power Outage in the Northeast

The largest blackout in U.S. history occurred on August 14, 2003, shortly after 2 p.m. (Eastern Daylight Time), when "a high-voltage power line in northern Ohio brushed against some overgrown trees and shut down—a fault, as it's known in the power industry. The line had softened under the heat of the high current coursing through it. Normally, the problem would have tripped an alarm in the control room of FirstEnergy Corporation, an Ohio-based utility company, but the alarm system failed.

"Over the next hour and a half, as system operators tried to understand what was happening, three other lines sagged into trees and switched off, forcing other power lines to shoulder an extra burden. Overtaxed, they cut out by 4:05 p.m., tripping a cascade of failures throughout southeastern Canada and eight northeastern states.

"All told, 50 million people lost power for up to two days. . . . The event contributed to at least 11 deaths and cost an estimated $6 billion."

(Minkel, 2008)

9. Expand your definition of staff; give volunteers assignments to fill in the gaps. The possibilities include managing public relations, videotaping and/or photographing the disaster, directing the evacuation of materials, fetching food and water, signing other volunteers in and out, providing security, and rounding up hard-to-find supplies.

10. Remember that the recovery process will require extreme patience. Travel will be difficult, and bridges, streets, and businesses will be closed. Open streets will close without notice. A 15-minute errand may take up to three hours or longer. Everyone in the impacted area is likely to need and compete for many of the same supplies.

—Nancy Kraft
Preservation Librarian
University of Iowa
Iowa City, IA

Biological Attacks

A biological attack is the deliberate release of germs or other biological agents that make people sick. These agents typically enter the body through the skin or are inhaled or ingested. Some agents, such as anthrax, are not contagious, while others, like smallpox, are easily transmitted from person to person.

Blackouts

Blackouts can be caused by many factors, including hurricanes, blizzards, extreme heat, and tornadoes.

Chemical or Toxic Leaks

Chemical or toxic leaks may be accidental or deliberate and are composed of the release of a toxic gas, liquid, or solid that adversely affects people and the environment. Sarin, a man-made chemical nerve agent, was used in an attack on the Tokyo subway in March 1995 that killed 13 people.

Earthquakes

While many perceive earthquakes to be a West Coast phenomenon, 45 states and territories are at moderate or high risk, some because of the New Madrid fault line in the central part of the United States. Devastating earthquakes in Asia and New Zealand in 2011 illustrate that these are an international problem.

Earthquakes in Christchurch, New Zealand

At 4:35 a.m. on September 4, 2010, the city of Christchurch (New Zealand) experienced an earthquake measuring 7.1 on the Richter Scale. The University of Canterbury was closed for two weeks following the earthquake, while buildings were checked for damage and structural integrity. Fortunately, the university was quiet at the time, with only a handful of students in the Central Library. The quake struck early on a Saturday morning during a vacation period.

The Central Library, which is an eleven-story building, made up of seven different structures, received damage to earthquake joints and structural damage to windows, ceilings, walls, and floors that required nearly six months to rectify. In addition, the library experienced significant damage to shelving, with bays of shelving collapsing like dominoes. Most of the approximately one million volumes ended up on the floor. The shelving company had to design new bracing for shelves that were not damaged and manufacture new shelving to replace the units that collapsed. Although the new shelving systems took months to be delivered and installed, safety was of prime concern. Library staff, academics, and students were promised that the new shelving would withstand a similar-sized earthquake without collapsing.

The other libraries on campus (Education, Engineering and Physical Sciences, Law, and Macmillan Brown Libraries) were closed until the buildings were checked, damage repaired, shelving replaced, and books and journals restacked.

It was apparent from the start that access to print collections would be severely restricted, so an appeal was made to major publishers and library vendors to provide additional access to digital information resources. All those asked provided unprecedented free access to electronic resources. While significant work was required to make these new resources discoverable through the library's federated search engine, the expanded access went a long way toward minimizing the impact of the closure of the libraries, and the Central Library in particular.

Fortunately, library staff members were able to relocate high-demand print collections from all closed libraries to those libraries which were open. As the floors of the Central Library were remediated, items on those floors which were reserved by students and staff were retrieved by library staff for pick-up at a library that was open.

A variety of communication channels was used to inform library customers about access to digital and print resources, including YouTube videos, university and library Facebook pages, student and staff forums, webpages, student magazines, and e-mail.

The earthquake was seen as an accelerator for change. The library had long tried to get funding for placing RFID tags in library volumes to enable efficient self-service borrowing. A business case was urgently prepared and approved by the University Council to take advantage of the need to reshelve the library's entire collections; tagging was added as a step in the reshelving process. The library also took this opportunity to rearrange the shelving sequence so that there was a more coherent pattern, starting with the Library of Congress classification A on the eleventh floor and moving down the tower to Z on the lower level of the Central Library.

The Central Library was the last library on campus to reopen after the September 2010 earthquake, opening on February 21, 2011, the first day of the new academic year. The following day a less powerful but more devastating earthquake struck Christchurch at 12:52 p.m. This earthquake, measuring 6.3 on the Richter Scale, resulted in 182 deaths in the central business district and decimated the city.

Amerithrax or Anthrax Investigation

Soon after the terrorist attacks of 9/11, letters laced with anthrax began appearing in the U.S. mail. Five Americans were killed and 17 were sickened in what became the worst biological attacks in U.S. history.

The ensuing investigation by the FBI [Federal Bureau of Investigation] and its partners—code-named "Amerithrax"—has been one of the largest and most complex in the history of law enforcement.

In August 2008, Department of Justice and FBI officials announced a breakthrough in the case and released documents and information showing that charges were about to be brought against Dr. Bruce Ivins, who took his own life before those charges could be filed. On February 19, 2010, the Justice Department, the FBI, and the U.S. Postal Inspection Service formally concluded the investigation into the 2001 anthrax attacks and issued an Investigative Summary.

(Reprinted from U.S. Federal Bureau of Investigation, 2011)

Although the university suffered much more structural damage in this earthquake compared to the impact of the September earthquake, the new shelving systems that replaced the damaged shelving stood up well, with no collapses. Books fell from shelves but could be reshelved as soon as buildings were declared safe to occupy.

The February earthquake badly affected the Law Library as well as the Central Library in a structural sense, although it was possible to reopen the Education and Macmillan Brown Libraries relatively quickly. The building housing the Engineering and Physical Sciences Library, which had been refurbished while closed following the September earthquake, remains closed, as it is compromised by unsafe buildings on either side of it.

Just as with the September 2010 quake, high-demand collections were relocated to open libraries. Again, publishers and library vendors provided additional access to digital information resources to supplement the licensed collections already held by the library.

A major difference, this time, was the need to close the campus for three weeks at the beginning of the academic year, which severely disrupted library inductions for new students. However, a benefit was a closer working relationship with the Flexible Learning Advisors who support academic staff in using the online learning space, a Moodle virtual classroom system. To supplement the loss of scheduled instruction sessions, librarians linked digital library resources and online tutorials to courses in Moodle.

During all of these events, library staff members have had to deal with personal tragedies, damage to their own homes, and problems with basic infrastructure such as water, sewage systems, and power. When possible, some worked from home; some volunteered to direct students to classrooms held in large marquees that had been erected on car parks. All had to cope with working in temporary accommodations and facing the daunting task of picking up and reshelving vast numbers of books multiple times. Another major aftershock closed the campus for three days in June 2011, with library books strewn on the floors yet again!

Business continuity planning and disaster recovery are no longer given lip service. All IT servers supporting library systems are in the primary data center with backup generators; many more online tutorials to support information literacy training are available; the importance of digital information resources has been highlighted, with staff and students using e-books, for example, more than before the earthquakes; AskLive, an online reference service, has shown its worth. More self-service options have been implemented, particularly in relation to in-person borrowing and interlibrary loans, to enable more library services to be accessed remotely. The library has had to store low-use material off-site, in commercial storage facilities, to make room for collections that have had to be relocated because of library closures, and this has led to more dialogue and cooperation between librarians and academic staff with regard to collection management. Project management skills have been honed.

Opportunities for change have been seized, as it would be a shame for a crisis not to have some silver linings!

—Sue McKnight, PhD
Pro-Vice Chancellor, Learning Resources
University of Canterbury
Christchurch, NZ

Explosions, Bomb Threats, and Active Shooters

Explosions and bomb threats can happen anywhere, but if they are part of a terrorist threat there are certain criteria that place an area at greater risk. Major landmarks, tourist attractions, large government institutions, and events such as the Super Bowl are prime targets for these types of threats. In 1995, 168 people were killed in the bombing of the Alfred P. Murrah Federal Building in Oklahoma City.

Active shooters are also becoming more common, especially on college and university campuses, such as the University of Texas shooting in September 2011 that is described in chapter 1 and the Virginia Tech incident in April 2007 addressed in chapter 5. Included on pages 80 and 81 are two examples of policies created by libraries to respond to a bomb threat and an active shooter.

Fires

According to FEMA, fires kill more than 4,000 and injure more than 20,000 people each year. Fires can occur at any time in a home, office, or public place.

Fire at Zimmerman Library, University of New Mexico

Just before 11:00 p.m. on Sunday, August 30, 2006, a fire started in the basement periodicals area of the University of New Mexico's (UNM) historic Zimmerman Library. The cause of the fire has never been officially announced; however, it is still under investigation as arson. Zimmerman Library, estimated as the most valuable resource in the state of New Mexico, is the main library on the UNM campus in Albuquerque and contains over one million education, humanities, and social sciences volumes. Zimmerman also houses special collections, technical services, and administration for the University Libraries (UL) system. Over 100 faculty and staff work in the facility. Within six minutes of the fire alarms sounding, library employees quickly and effectively evacuated the students preparing for final projects, papers, and exams that evening. The fire department arrived and extinguished the fire, which was confined to a corner of the basement periodicals area; however, lighting and smoke detectors were melted, the flooring and walls were destroyed, and even the reinforced metal shelving warped and collapsed. The blaze destroyed about 30,000 periodicals in subject areas including history and ethnic studies. Some subject areas adjacent to the fire, including geography, anthropology, religion, philosophy, political science, and education, were severely damaged. Because of smoke from the fire and water damage sustained as the fire was being put out, most furnishings and computers in the 44,000-square-foot basement had to be replaced. In addition, the intense heat from the fire melted wiring in electrical cabinets serving all floors on the east side of the building and damaged the first floor reference area. Smoke as well as some ash and soot were distributed throughout the 287,000-square-foot building.

The UL's *Emergency Preparedness and Recovery Plan* was instrumental in guiding the initial response and later recovery efforts. Just over a year before the

University of Virginia Health Sciences Library
Telephone Bomb Threat Checklist

TIME: Call received _____ a.m./p.m. Terminated _____ a.m./p.m. DATE: _____ / _____ / _____

EXACT WORDING OF THE THREAT

_____

_____

_____

Sex of Caller: _____ Race: _____

Age: _____ Length of Call: _____

Number at which call is received: _____

QUESTIONS YOU SHOULD ASK

A. When is bomb going to explode?   D. What kind of bomb is it?   G. Why?

B. Where is the bomb right now?   E. What will cause it to explode?   H. What is your address?

C. What does it look like?   F. Did you place the bomb?   I. What is your name?

VOICE DESCRIPTION

___ Calm   ___ Lisp   ___ Soft   ___ Deep breathing   ___ Distinct

___ Nasal   ___ Slow   ___ Ragged   ___ Crying   ___ Accent

___ Angry   ___ Raspy   ___ Loud   ___ Cracking voice   ___ Slurred

___ Stutter   ___ Rapid   ___ Clearing throat   ___ Normal   ___ Familiar

___ Excited   ___ Deep   ___ Laughter   ___ Disguised   ___ Whispered

Recognize Voice? If so, who do you think it was? _____

BACKGROUND SOUNDS

___ Street noises   ___ Clear   ___ House noises

___ Factory machinery   ___ PA system   ___ Long distance

___ Crockery   ___ Static   ___ Motor

___ Animal noises   ___ Music   ___ Booth

___ Voices   ___ Local   ___ Office machinery

___ Other: _____

THREAT LANGUAGE

___ Well-spoken   ___ Foul   ___ Irrational

___ Incoherent   ___ Taped   ___ Message read by threat maker

Date: _____ / _____ / _____

Name: _____

Position: _____

Phone number: _____

Source: Daniel T. Wilson, Associate Director for Collection Management and Access Services, University of Virginia Claude Moore Health Sciences Library, Charlottesville, VA.

The Texas Medical Center Library
Active Shooter Checklist

Securing immediate area

- ❑ Lock and barricade doors
- ❑ Turn off all lights
- ❑ Close blinds
- ❑ Block windows
- ❑ Turn off radios and computer monitors
- ❑ Keep occupants calm, quiet, and out of sight
- ❑ Keep yourself out of sight and take adequate cover or protection (e.g., concrete walls, desks, filing cabinets) that may protect you from bullets
- ❑ Silence cell phones
- ❑ Place signs in exterior windows to identify the location of injured people

Moving an area to unsecured status

- ❑ Consider risks before area is unsecured
- ❑ Remember, the shooter will not stop until engaged by an outside force
- ❑ Attempts to rescue people should be made only if they can be accomplished without further endangering people inside a secured area
- ❑ Consider the safety of masses versus the safety of few
- ❑ If doubt exists for the safety of the individuals inside the room, the area should remain secure

Contacting authorities

- ❑ Use Emergency 9-911 (must dial 9 for an outside line then 911)
- ❑ Be aware that the 911 system could be overwhelmed
- ❑ If you are afraid of being detected, e-mail or text someone to call 911 on your behalf

What to report

- ❑ Your specific location/building name and office/room number
- ❑ Number of people at your specific location
- ❑ Number of injured and types of injuries
- ❑ Location(s) of assailant(s)
- ❑ Number of assailants
- ❑ Description of assailant(s) including race, gender, clothing, and physical features
- ❑ Types of weapons
- ❑ Identity of assailant(s), if known

Source: Jesse Gonzalez, Assistant Director, Circulation, The Texas Medical Center Library, Houston, TX.

Zimmerman Library fire, the plan had been extensively updated and enhanced after it was used when a flood ravaged the lower level of the UL's Centennial Science and Engineering Library, resulting in the loss of over 20,000 maps and the remediation of the entire bottom floor. Even as smoke from the fire was billowing out from the Zimmerman Library building, the Deputy Dean and Facilities Manager, who were the first library administrators on the scene, began executing the plan's phone tree to contact other members of the UL's Disaster Response Assistance Team (DRAT), consisting of administrators and managers, and other UL employees. DRAT met just nine hours later at 8:00 a.m. to begin taking action to establish alternate services to meet user needs, to identify and assign alternative work spaces for displaced library employees, and to assess the damage to and plan for the remediation of the library's collections, facilities, and equipment.

Priority one was to provide communication with and uninterrupted services to UL users. To accomplish this goal, DRAT members developed a webpage that included current information, with an FAQ section; information tables under tents were set up and staffed for a week outside the entrances to Zimmerman Library; reference and information tables staffed by librarians using laptop computers were placed in the campus Student Union Building (SUB); hours of operation at the SUB and at other branch libraries were extended through final exams week to provide safe locations for students to study and complete final projects and papers; print materials on reserve at Zimmerman Library were moved to another branch library; and a paging system to retrieve books from Zimmerman Library's second and third floors (until the facility could be reopened) was designed. The UL's substantial collection of electronic journals and expedited interlibrary loan service aided students to complete their end-of-semester assignments as well as for students and faculty to conduct research until the print periodicals and microforms were made available again when the basement level reopened to the public. Within hours of containing the fire, a local company was on-site with air-scrubbers and other equipment to begin the cleanup. A few days later, a major international disaster restoration company was hired to remove, freeze-dry as needed, clean, deodorize, and store at its out-of-state facility all periodical, microform, and other collections located in the basement. Sorting and moving this vast amount of collections and debris from the basement were logistically challenging and time-consuming. However, working together, DRAT members and other library employees, other campus entities, local construction and cleaning companies, and a major restoration company oversaw the full renovation of the Zimmerman Library basement level (which had to be stripped to the concrete walls and rebuilt), the repair of the heat- and smoke-damaged first floor, and the painstaking cleaning and repair of the entire building.

Recovery from this level of destruction was a monumental task. It was nearly a week before the State Fire Marshal released Zimmerman Library to UNM officials because it had been designated a crime scene and was under investigation for arson. It took another week before cleaning was completed in some areas so that a few employees could move back into Zimmerman Library and still more weeks before it could partially reopen to the public on June 26, 2006. The damaged reference area on the first floor could not reopen until January 16, 2007, and the basement level, which housed the education, humanities, and social sciences print periodicals and the microforms collection as well as technical services employees, could not reopen until March 24, 2008. The basement would have reopened as early as November 2007 if a major water pipe had not broken on October 31, 2007, during reconstruction, flooding the basement and requiring additional remediation. An official reopening celebration was held on April 30, 2008, on the two-year anniversary of the fire.

As devastating and emotionally charged as library disasters are, they can provide many opportunities and valuable lessons, a few of which include:

- Create, regularly update, and widely distribute a comprehensive *Emergency Preparedness and Disaster Recovery Plan* with emergency contact information, roles and responsibilities of disaster team members, procedures and resources, locations of disaster supplies, salvage priorities by location, library building information with floor plans, and any other information appropriate for the specific library. Make the plan available both on the Internet and in paper format for situations when Internet access is not possible.
- Precontract with a disaster restoration company before disaster strikes to arrange the best terms and prices. This contract can save time and avoid confusion later.
- Throughout the disaster event, communicate regularly with employees, users, other campus entities, donors, vendors, disaster restoration/construction companies, insurance companies, the media, and appropriate others. Though time-consuming, well-timed and well-placed communication greatly enhances implementation of the plan and overall recovery.
- Facilities can be rebuilt and reconfigured to better serve user populations in ways that might not have been otherwise possible with dwindling library budgets.
- Accept and acknowledge emotional aftershocks. Respect the need for employees and others to express emotions and provide assistance as needed.
- Celebrate small and large victories at every stage of the recovery process.

—Fran Wilkinson
Deputy Dean, University Libraries
Chair, UL's Disaster Response and Assistance Team
UL's Interim Dean, July 1, 2006–July 31, 2007
University of New Mexico
Albuquerque, NM

Flooding

Flooding, the most common disaster in the United States, can happen anywhere, developing slowly over a period of days or occurring almost instantly as a flash flood. In addition to weather events, plumbing issues and malfunctions with HVAC systems or fire protection systems such as sprinklers can also cause flooding in a residence or workplace.

USGS National Landslide Hazards Program

According to the U.S. Geological Survey (USGS), landslides constitute a major geologic hazard because they occur in all 50 states and cause $1 billion to $2 billion in damages each year. Expansion of urban and recreational developments into hillside areas leads to more people being exposed to landslides each year. Landslides often occur in connection with other major natural disasters such as earthquakes, volcanoes, wildfires, and floods. The USGS has created the National Landslide Hazards Program (http://landslides.usgs.gov/) to reduce long-term losses from landslides by improving understanding of the causes of ground failure and suggesting mitigation strategies.

Nuclear Accident in Fukushima, Japan

Two reactor buildings once painted in a cheery sky blue loom over the Fukushima Dai-ichi nuclear power plant. Their roofs are blasted away, their crumbled concrete walls reduced to steel frames.

In their shadow, plumbers, electricians, and truck drivers, sometimes numbering in the thousands, go dutifully about their work, all clad from head to toe in white hazmat suits. Their job—cleaning up the worst nuclear disaster since Chernobyl—will take decades to complete.

Reporters, also in radiation suits, visited the ravaged facility Saturday for the first time since Japan's

Continued on p. 85

Flooding at the Sidney Memorial Public Library

In the last week of June 2006, unprecedented flooding struck central Pennsylvania and the southern tier of Upstate New York. In a very short window of time, a number of storm systems dumped between 8 and 15 inches of rain on already saturated ground. In the village of Sidney, New York, the event was referred to as a 450-year flood event. The village was under a state of emergency for days, and the National Guard was called in to assist.

The public library in Sidney is located on the aptly named River Street, and the library property is bounded by the Susquehanna River. During the flood event, the 5,000-square-foot basement of the library, which housed the boiler room, oil tank storage, book and materials storage, the staff lounge, a meeting room, two restrooms, an elevator, and staff office space, as well as the computer server and phone and network connections, was filled with over 5 feet of water. By mobilizing community volunteers and staff, the library was open and functioning within 10 days of the flood's peak.

The most useful tools during the disaster response were an up-to-date disaster plan, a well-informed staff, and good relationships with key community members (such as the mayor, the fire and police chiefs, and the school superintendent) and the larger community.

Key lessons learned included:

- It is important to document.

    o If you have an up-to-date inventory list, it's easier to identify what you've lost.
    o A photo can be worth a thousand words.

- Use the unique gifts and talents of volunteers and staff.

    o If they can't help with the cleanup, find tasks they can perform.
    o Keep everyone well-informed and involved.

- Celebrate the successes and victories.

    o It's morale-boosting.
    o Progress helps to keep discouragement at bay.

After the adrenalin subsides and the momentum of the initial response diminishes, it's important to try to maintain a positive outlook. It may take months and months of filling out forms and follow-up before things will be back to "normal." We found the most useful tools during the aftermath of the disaster response to be a good sense of humor, persistence, and patience.

−Mary Grace Flaherty
Director, 2002–2008
Sidney Memorial Public Library
Sidney, NY

Hurricanes/Typhoons

Hurricanes and typhoons are severe storms that heavily impact a specific geographic area, and typically other areas are subsequently affected by these weather events. For example, many hurricanes striking the states that border the Gulf of Mexico spawn storms that travel across the country causing widespread damage and power outages. In addition to the direct effects of a hurricane on the library itself, the library can, in fact, be called on to help the community, as was the case with Houston Public Library following Hurricane Katrina.

Houston Public Library Post-Katrina

Houston was an epicenter for the evacuees from New Orleans after Hurricane Katrina destroyed large portions of the city. Thousands were evacuated to the Astrodome in Houston, and when that was full, Bill White, Mayor of the City of Houston, prepared to open the George R. Brown Convention Center to additional evacuees. He called a meeting of all department directors, including the interim director of the Houston Public Library (HPL), Toni Lambert. This was very important because she was able to secure a place for the library when discussions focused on the services to be offered to the tired, overwhelmed evacuees who were about to arrive.

I was eager to help and was put in charge of creating a temporary branch of the HPL in the convention center. With help from many, many wonderful staff and volunteers we built a library at the George R. Brown Convention Center where we went from an empty ballroom to a fully stocked temporary library in 24 hours. Shelving arrived from a temporally closed HPL location and was installed. AT&T installed an Internet connection so that HPL and its customers could be connected. HPL's IT department delivered 24 computers that were scheduled for branch replacements and wired a router so that every computer had Internet access through the library servers. A community group brought 12 personal computers with DOS games installed on them to entertain the children. Volunteers brought thousands of books of every type you could imagine. A call to IKEA brought furniture for a children's play area. Toys from an HPL initiative added activities for young children, Target provided games for them to play, and library staff volunteered to come in and provide services. Temporary library cards were issued to allow evacuees access to library resources for six weeks. Staff at the Central Library began putting together resources that the evacuees would need. Movie licenses were purchased so that HPL could show films in the Convention Center.

Evacuees arrived by the thousands. They were very tired and very scared and needed a way to figure out how to deal with the mess their lives had just become. The first day was just about recovery—tired parents looking for something for children to do; traumatized children working through exhaustion and fear; volunteers everywhere trying to be helpful. Everyone, including me, was trying to figure out what the rules were and how we were going to do this. What began as a race to set up and figure things out became a daily adventure in helping people find the information they needed to start over, providing a place for children to be children, and serving as a teen hangout, especially in the evenings when they just needed someplace to call their own for a while.

The biggest need was Internet access for communication, résumés, job applications, finding bank accounts, apartments, phone numbers, and the list goes on. Ways that HPL helped evacuees at the George R. Brown Convention Center temporary library included the following:

Continued from p. 84

worst tsunami in centuries swamped the plant March 11, causing reactor explosions and meltdowns and turning hundreds of square miles of countryside into a no-man's-land.

Eight months later, the plant remains a shambles. Mangled trucks, flipped over by the power of the wave, still clutter its access roads. Rubble remains strewn where it fell. Pools of water cover parts of the once immaculate campus.

Tens of thousands of the plant's former neighbors may never be able to go home. And just as Hiroshima and Nagasaki became icons of the horrors of nuclear weapons, Fukushima has become the new rallying cry of the global anti-nuclear energy movement.

Yet this picture is one of progress, Japanese officials say. It has taken this long to make the plant stable enough to allow Saturday's tour, which included representatives of the Japanese and international media—including the Associated Press. Officials expect to complete an early but important step toward cleaning up the accident by the end of the year.

(Reprinted from Guttenfelder and Talmadge, 2011)

Hazards Associated with Volcanic Eruptions

Debris flows, or lahars, are slurries of muddy debris and water caused by mixing of solid debris with water, melted snow, or ice. Lahars destroyed houses, bridges, and logging trucks during the May 1980 eruption of Mount St. Helens, and have inundated other valleys around Cascade volcanoes during prehistoric eruptions. Lahars at Nevado del Ruiz volcano, Colombia, in 1985 killed more than 23,000 people. At Mount Ranier, lahars

Continued on p. 87

- One fun 30 minutes I helped three gentlemen find companies looking for welders, let them use my cell phone to make appointments for job interviews, looked on the giant city map donated by Key Map and gave them directions, and then identified a few good apartment complexes in the same area as the jobs and off they went. They found jobs at the first company they talked to and secured an apartment in the same afternoon with a call from the employer.
- HPL helped an elderly woman find her relatives and got her in contact with them.
- One woman had just had her relief funds deposited into a bank account at an institution that was underwater. Staff had to figure out which federal agency controlled that institution and get her on the list of people to be notified when account information became available. We then spoke to a local bank that thought it might be able to help her. Since the money had been deposited electronically the bank thought it might be able to transfer the funds to another account electronically.

The evacuees were in need of a constant connection to the outside world. Internet access was the key to assistance, housing, bank accounts, communication with family and friends, jobs, and everything you need when your world evaporates. Lessons learned here allowed HPL to provide better services to our citizens when Hurricane Ike hit the Houston area. We found once again that what people needed most was access to online resources and a place to charge their cell phones and computers. The library is practically the only place in the community that can offer these services, implement a plan to manage the influx successfully, and possess the capability to be flexible and understanding.

−Sandy Farmer
Manager, Central Youth Services
Houston Public Library
Houston, TX

Landslides

Landslides have a wide geographic distribution and can be catastrophic events. Significant service interruptions can be the result because of employee shortages, closure of public facilities, and resource scarcities.

Nuclear Threats

Nuclear threats that were present during the Cold War have diminished, but the possibility remains that nuclear weapons or material may be used in a terrorist attack. Leaks or accidents at nuclear facilities are also a major concern with the potential of causing significant environmental damage, long-term health consequences, and loss of life.

Pandemics

A pandemic occurs when a highly contagious disease such as influenza travels over large geographic areas. Pandemics can strike anywhere and cause service interruptions by creating an employee shortage when staff members fall ill or by initiating closure of public facilities like libraries in an attempt to control exposure.

Tornadoes

Tornadoes are nature's most violent storms, as illustrated throughout the United States in 2011. Although technological advances have significantly improved the ability to predict and track tornadic activity, tornadoes can appear suddenly and may be invisible until dust and debris are picked up or a funnel cloud appears. Conditions such as heavy rain can also hide funnels, making the threat difficult to see.

Joplin Tornado

When my husband, Phil, and I went into the basement for the tornado warning on May 22, 2011, we expected the usual event: Go to the basement with our corgi, Mookie, and a few things we grab on the way, leave the door open for the cats to come down if they choose to, hang out until the warning expires, then resume our evening. Phil and I grew up in "Tornado Alley" and have been through countless tornado warnings with no incident, so why would May 22 be any different?

We began to realize this tornado warning was different when the world outside our basement window turned green, but we still expected to resume our normal life. The likelihood of a tornado hitting our house is very small, after all, and the likelihood of that tornado being an EF5 that destroys everything is even smaller.

Shortly after the world turned green, the wind picked up to the point of being scary and we decided to move to the little room under our basement stairs that houses our water heater. I was two steps from the door to the room when we lost power, and Phil had just closed the door when the glass started breaking.

As we huddled under the stairs with one arm around each other and one arm holding Mookie, everything around us and above us became chaotic. Our ears popped, we could feel wind on our backs (part of the staircase is uncovered and open to the rest of the basement), and we could hear thuds, thumps, and breaking glass, all mixed in with a huge, ground-shaking rumble that lasted a split second and forever all at once.

When the noises and the wind lessened and then stopped, all three of us were covered in dust and insulation. We emerged from the room under the stairs to the evening sky. We knew then that our roof and our kitchen were gone. Phil ventured up the basement stairs and told me the rest of the house was gone too. Then he looked around and said the rest of the neighborhood was gone.

All external walls of our house were swept clean away, as was the roof (we still don't know where it landed). The only part of our home that remained was the interior walls, and to call them "standing" is an overstatement.

Beyond our house were skeletal trees that had once been lush and green, power lines, overturned cars, piles of rubble that had once been our neighbors' houses, and dazed people emerging from the wreckage of their homes. As far as the eye could see to the north, east, south, and west was destruction.

Once Phil and I knew we were okay and our neighbors were okay, the decision making began. Any semblance of an emergency plan Phil and I had was in serious

Continued from p. 86
have also been produced by major landslides that apparently were neither triggered nor accompanied by eruptive activity. Lahars can travel many tens of miles in a period of hours, destroying everything in their paths.

Tephra (ash and coarser debris) is composed of fragments of magma or rock blown apart by gas expansion. Tephra can cause roofs to collapse, endanger people with respiratory problems, and damage machinery. Tephra can clog machinery, severely damage aircraft, cause respiratory problems, and short out power lines up to hundreds of miles downwind of eruptions. Explosions may also throw large rocks up to a few miles. Falling blocks killed people at Galeras Volcano in Colombia in 1992, and at Mount Etna, Italy, in 1979.

Pyroclastic surges and flows are hot, turbulent clouds of tephra (surges) or dense, turbulent mixtures of tephra and gas (known as flows). Pyroclastic flows and surges can travel more than a hundred miles per hour and incinerate or crush most objects in their path. Though most extend only a few miles, a pyroclastic surge at Mount St. Helens in 1980 extended 18 miles (28 km) and killed 57 people. Pyroclastic surges at El Chichón volcano in Mexico in 1982 killed 2,000 people, and pyroclastic flows at Mount Unzen, Japan, in June 1991 killed 43 people."

(Reprinted from Volcano Hazards Program, 2010)

Special Libraries Association (SLA) Joins Tsunami Relief Effort

Everyone has seen the devastation caused by the tsunami/sea wave in southern Asia. The overwhelming loss of life and property will affect that region of the world for years to come. But the world is responding with aid and support, and SLA hopes to energize the global community of information professionals to get involved.

Staff at SLA Headquarters is embarking on an initiative to serve as an information clearinghouse for our community. This initiative will focus on two critical areas of need:

- Providing direction to members and SLA unit leaders for immediate financial support for the disaster relief effort. A collection of contacts for relief agencies and charities that are committed to the relief effort is now available online. SLA Information Services Staff selected lists from the governments of the top five nations most populated by SLA members, plus the nations affected by this awful natural disaster. We encourage all SLA members and units to consider making a contribution to

Continued on p. 89

jeopardy at that point. We had no way of knowing how wide or long the path was or where we were in relation to its borders. Our cars had been destroyed or buried under rubble (we didn't have keys to them anyway), and our cell phones didn't work beyond an occasional text or Facebook update getting through.

Without really having time to process what happened to us or to our home, we immediately had to decide where we would find shelter and how we would get there. Once we had shelter for Sunday night, we had to start thinking about longer term shelter. Phil needed a tetanus shot and I was 18 weeks pregnant, so we had to find a doctor to check us both out (our baby was perfectly fine). We had to call our insurance company and FEMA. We had to decide how to protect ourselves from identity theft. We had to decide when and how we would go back to the wreckage to see what we could salvage. When we did go back, we had to decide what was worth keeping and what we would let the tornado have. We had to find a place to store what we salvaged until we had more permanent arrangements. We had to start thinking about what we wanted to do with our property—rebuild or sell the lot? We had to decide when to go back to work. We had to find a car to get us there. Most of all, we had to decide how to let other people help us.

We had to decide so many things within the first weeks that it was difficult to function. At first, the decision-making process overwhelms any chance to mentally recover from the disaster. We had no choice but to continue to decide things—from big to small. We had to move forward.

As I write this, we haven't quite reached the two-month mark. The decision-making process continues. Now that most of the immediate decisions have been made, Phil and I have been able to step back some and process what happened. Even though it has been weeks since the actual event, we still have a lot of mental and emotional recovering to do. That process is just as slow as the physical rebuilding process.

Phil and I both took some time off work immediately after the tornado, as did many people at my library. I am one of nine library employees who lost everything. In a staff of 45, nine such losses are felt pretty significantly. Thankfully, of the nine we only had two injuries and neither was severe. The library staff and the library board have been very generous since the tornado—helping cover shifts, forgiving days missed because of the storm, starting a staff relief fund, and above all else providing us with sympathetic ears once we were able to tell our stories. I could not have asked for better coworkers than the people at the Joplin Public Library.

Being back at work was difficult at first but has become a chance to feel productive and helpful in the midst of the chaos and helplessness. I feel like I'm directly contributing to Joplin's recovery when I hear others' stories and help ease their lives while they are in the library. Working with my teens during our Summer Reading Program is a precious experience this summer. All the teens have been affected by the tornado. They lost their homes or their schools or their friends, but being together at the library interacting with people their own age who know exactly what it's like seems to be as good for them as it is for me to see.

On the whole, life is looking better, and we are returning to a sense of normalcy. Phil and I have a contract on a new home (with a basement) in Joplin and plans for how to furnish it since only three pieces of our furniture survived the tornado. Our baby, a boy, is still doing very well. We have just enough time to get his nursery in order before he arrives in October. We still haven't decided definitively what to do with our old lot, but we will prepare the property to be rebuilt with the basement that saved our lives. We have also discussed how to prepare for the unexpected from now on—no longer do we take the stance of "the likelihood of this happening is so small that we don't need to worry about it."

The important things walked out of that basement on May 22 or, in the case of our cats, were found alive and well on May 23. The rest of what we found after our lives were laid bare by the tornado is bonus. The community in Joplin is strong. It will come back and Phil and I and our son will be right here helping it do just that.

−Cari Rerat
Teen Librarian
Joplin Public Library
Joplin, MO

Tsunamis

Tsunamis are enormous oceanic waves that are caused by an underground disturbance such as an earthquake or volcanic eruption. Tsunamis can reach heights of almost 100 feet and speeds of almost 600 miles per hour.

Volcanoes

Volcanoes occur when pressure builds up within a volcano's molten rock sending forth lava flows, poisonous gases, and flying rock and ash that can travel hundreds of miles downwind, contributing to property damage, poor air quality, and difficult environmental conditions.

Conclusion

The purpose of this chapter was twofold: first, emphasizing the importance of personal preparedness and incorporating these elements into any library disaster planning and, second, raising awareness of specific threats and sharing lessons learned in responding to those threats.

References

Guttenfelder, David, and Eric Talmadge. 2011. "Japan Fukushima Reactor: Eight Months after Nuclear Disaster, Plant Remains in Shambles." *Huff Post: World*, November 11. http://www .huffingtonpost.com/2011/11/12/japan-fukushima-reactor-e_n_1089900.html#s469932.

Minkel, J. R. 2008. "The 2003 Northeast Blackout—Five Years Later." *Scientific American*, August 13. http://www.scientificamerican.com/ article.cfm?id=2003-blackout-five-years-later&print=true.

"Pandemic Flu History: 1918–1919." 2014. Flu.gov. Accessed April 2. http://www.flu.gov/pandemic/history/.

Continued from p. 88

this effort. We also ask that you please share your commitment with SLA. Once you've made a contribution, let us know at communications@sla.org, so that we may appropriately recognize you for your generosity.

- Serving as a conduit for (a) educating members of our community on the needs of libraries in the affected region for the purpose of rebuilding or restoration; and (b) directing information, resources, and expertise to persons in the affected region who will guide library rebuilding or restoration. This will be developed over the first several months of 2005, so that an effective collection of resources can be made available.

This initiative serves as a way for all of us to contribute to a global effort; to help those left behind in this horrible experience; and to aid an entire region of the world in moving forward from absolute devastation. Look for more details on this initiative here in *Connections* and in *Information Outlook*.

The staff and leadership of SLA continue to keep the victims and their families in our thoughts.

(Reprinted from Special Libraries Association, 2005)

Special Libraries Association (SLA). 2005. "SLA Joins Tsunami Relief Effort." SLA. http://www.sla.org/content/resources/tsunamirelief.cfm (page discontinued).

United Way of Greater Houston. 2011. "Are You Prepared for Hurricane Season?" United Way of Greater Houston. http://unitedwayhouston .org/?NewsID=555.

U.S. Federal Bureau of Investigation (FBI). 2011. "Amerithrax or Anthrax Investigation." FBI. http://www.fbi.gov/about-us/history/ famous-cases/anthrax-amerithrax/amerithrax-investigation.

U.S. Government Accountability Office (GAO). 2011. "National Preparedness: DHS and HHS Can Further Strengthen Coordination for Chemical, Biological, Radiological, and Nuclear Risk Assessments." GAO. http://www.gao.gov/products/GAO-11-606.

Volcano Hazards Program. 2010. "Frequently Asked Questions about Volcanic Hazards." U.S. Geological Survey. Last modified September 2. http://volcanoes.usgs.gov/about/faq/faqhazards.php.

Leveraging the Library

On January 20, 2011, the American Library Association (ALA) announced that efforts by Senator Jack Reed (D-RI) resulted in a change to a Federal Emergency Management Agency (FEMA) policy that allows libraries to be designated as temporary relocation facilities during major disasters and emergencies under the FEMA Public Assistance Program (http://connect .ala.org/node/127510). Section 403 of the Stafford Act authorizes FEMA to provide federal assistance to meet immediate threats to life and property resulting from a crisis. The act allows for the provision of temporary facilities for essential community services when it is related to saving lives and protecting or preserving property, public health, and safety. The ALA press release quoted Emily Sheketoff, executive director of the ALA Washington office as saying, "In times of disaster, libraries strive to ensure the public has access to the resources and services they need, but prior to this policy change libraries were not specifically included in the list of eligible public facilities" (American Library Association, 2011).

Recognizing libraries as an essential part of a community's disaster planning and recovery efforts is a major step forward. While it will come as no surprise to many librarians who have experienced a local, regional, or national disaster that there are numerous roles information professionals are suited to fill in times of crisis, being formally recognized in documents such as the Stafford Act highlights the potential contributions of libraries in preparedness, recovery, and response.

A number of experiences already illustrate the willingness of librarians to think outside the box and move beyond traditional library activities to meet community needs following a disaster. Librarians have been found driving a FEMA bus for relocated hospital staff members following Hurricane Katrina; serving in a Joint Information Center following weather events in the Texas Gulf Coast; acting as conduits to information on finding misplaced family members; accessing valuable national, regional, and local assistance resources; and participating in local command centers. But, according to a study by Zach and McKnight, the focus of library disaster planning has most often been turned inward toward the institution rather than outward toward

IN THIS CHAPTER:

✓ Traditional Roles

✓ Nontraditional Roles

✓ Conclusion

✓ References

the community. They speculate that information professionals have often missed opportunities to provide essential support for a variety of users following disasters. Information professionals are uniquely equipped to provide specialized assistance to both users responding to the disaster as well as those who have been directly impacted by the event (Zach and McKnight, 2010).

This chapter examines traditional and nontraditional roles for librarians in the aftermath of a disaster. As addressed in chapter 6, it is important to reiterate here that all staff members should have a personal preparedness plan to protect themselves and their families so that they can concentrate on the library after an event. It must also be noted that, in the case of a large incident, many library staff members will be engaged with personal challenges such as locating missing family members, salvaging a home, or dealing with displacement after an evacuation. The library's plan should include contingencies for such staff shortages.

As illustrated by many of the library stories shared in chapter 6, a disaster can provide libraries with new opportunities to market current and new services while raising the library's visibility to management, local authorities, first responders, and the community as a whole. By looking for the silver lining and thinking creatively, many libraries found that after a disaster community members had a heightened awareness of the value of staff, collections, and services. For example, following Hurricane Ike, many public libraries in the greater Houston area had record library card registration and increased circulation, and they added new customers who continue to use the library to this day. Many of these people came to libraries to charge cell phones and laptops, others to escape the lack of electricity at home, others to get help locating recovery assistance, and some just to relieve the boredom of being homebound for an extended period of time.

Traditional Roles

Recent events show that there are many roles that librarians can play in planning for and recovering from a disaster. In 2007, Robin Featherstone, a National Library of Medicine Associate, collected stories about roles that librarians can assume in emergency and disaster planning, preparedness, response, and recovery (Featherstone, Lyons, and Ruffin, 2008). Published in the *Journal of the Medical Library Association*, this oral history sought to describe both expected and unanticipated roles performed by librarians during and in the aftermath of disasters. The authors' conclusion was that librarians made significant contributions to preparedness and recovery activities surrounding disasters. This project increased the understanding of librarian roles and underscored the value of building and maintaining collaborative relationships with local, state, and federal disaster management agencies. This chapter illustrates ways for librarians to demonstrate their worth in the event of a disaster. Much of this information is based on the study mentioned and incorporates many librarians' personal stories.

Librarians, as professionals, excel in the role of collecting and organizing information and then making it available to those who need or want it. Following a disaster, information needs often increase, the demographics of the primary user populations may change dramatically, and unique challenges surrounding the protection, restoration, and accessibility of collections may be introduced. How can libraries not only meet these challenges but also embrace them and capitalize on new opportunities?

Bellaire (Texas) Public Library Recovery Efforts from Hurricane Ike

The library opened on Tuesday, September 16 (three days after the hurricane struck), with no evening hours and extended hours on Friday. By Saturday, regular hours were established and maintained.

Damage to the library was limited to no power until Monday, partial power Monday, Tuesday, and part of Wednesday, with complete power restored at 2:00 p.m. on Wednesday. A roof leak in the stairwell area caused several ceiling tiles to fall, but water damage was not widespread throughout the library.

During the time the library was open and available, the staff fielded many questions by telephone and from walk-ins. These questions included:

- Is the water supply safe?
- Is the library open? How long?
- Can I charge my laptop? Phone?
- May I have city hall's phone number?
- Is Randall's (grocery store) open? Do they have power?
- Is there trash pickup today?
- Do you have Internet? WiFi?
- Will wireless work after the library closes?
- What food places are open?
- What other libraries are open?
- Where can I change license plates?
- What time is it?
- What area gas stations are open?
- Do you have electricity? Air conditioning? Fax machine?
- Will I be charged fines for dates you were closed?
- What are city curfew times?

FAQs were posted on the front door of the library. Many people were seeking means to charge electronics, since the greater Houston area was without power for literally weeks. Internet access was also important.

Staff set up charging stations and monitored computer use to offer as many people access to the Internet as possible. Children's movies were shown, and board games were provided to help parents entertain their children. The children's librarian held her regularly scheduled infant and preschool storytimes and also maintained schedules for movie showings and crafts. New books and DVDs were quickly cataloged and made available for circulation to help people get their mind off the storm situation.

Over the week we observed many who brought their own laptops in order to access the WiFi network (at one time staff counted 30 personal laptops in the library). Several people were working, students were connected to school, teachers were checking on their classes, many were paying bills, several FEMA applications were made, insurance information was sought, and social sites (Facebook, MySpace, etc.) as well as online games were quite popular. Library staff members were lenient with fines and renewals. Perhaps most important, the library became a gathering place where members of the community, neighbors and strangers alike, met to share Ike stories.

—Mary Alford Cohrs
Director
Bellaire Public Library
Bellaire, TX

Information Disseminators

Putting information in the hands of people who need it is the core tenet of what libraries and library employees are all about. With regard to preparedness and recovery and response efforts, these skills enable librarians to bring much needed information to their general audience or to the community at large.

- Information resources for displaced persons: People who are forced to flee an area due to a large-scale event such as a hurricane or an earthquake may have unique and urgent information needs. In recent years, public librarians have excelled at providing assistance in connecting to school, paying bills online, completing FEMA applications, finding insurance information, and locating displaced family members and friends.
- Emergency print medical resources: When a major event occurs large numbers of people may be relocated to mass shelters, as was the case after Hurricane Katrina. Evacuees arrive with a variety of health conditions, no medical records, and often hard-to-identify medications. Health-care professionals are often taken out of their realm of expertise, such as pediatricians treating geriatric patients and surgeons providing primary care. Basic print resources such as the *Physicians' Desk Reference* and the *Merck Manual of Diagnosis and Therapy* are vital for treating these patients effectively. In this increasingly digital age it is also important to remember that print materials are reliable when electricity and access to the Internet are not.
- Emergency electronic medical resources: Health professionals caring for people evacuating to Houston after Hurricane Katrina did have access to electricity and the Internet. For that reason, electronic medical resources were available in both of the major shelters. Computers were set up in both shelter locations, and librarians negotiated with vendors to allow health professionals not covered in current license agreements to access proprietary databases and journals.

Institutional Supporters

Librarians can offer many services before, during, and after a disaster, including use of the library as a Command or Joint Information Center, a central location for institutional announcements and updates, or a resource center for displaced persons. Library staff can also provide valuable assistance and feedback related to the creation and maintenance of an institution-wide disaster plan.

- Command or Joint Information Center: Often, the library is situated in the center of a campus or institution. This location, along with the resources available, such as public computers, telephones, scanners/copiers/fax machines, meeting rooms, and restrooms, make the library a convenient place to house the Command Center, Joint Information Center, or media hub. The access to computers, Internet connectivity, staff expertise, and other resources position the library in a perfect spot for obtaining and disseminating information.
- Hub for FEMA and/or other first responder groups: Because libraries are often located near other vital agencies (police/fire departments, city hall, university administration, etc.) the library facilities may be connected to high-priority local grids considered essential for maintaining vital infrastructure. With such infrastructure support the library can serve as the hub for those offering assistance to individuals affected by a disaster.
- Location for disseminating institutional announcements and updates: As with the first two examples, the library can also serve as a central location for disseminating vital information such as status updates, closure and reopening announcements regarding public facilities and schools, location of points of distribution (PODs) for food and water, discontinuation and restoration of essential services, and updates on the current situation.

Community Supporters

In everyday roles, librarians serve as community supporters in many ways. For example, public librarians offer resources to those who are unemployed during the current recession. School librarians offer research assistance to students required to write a term paper. Medical librarians offer vital resources necessary to improve patient care, research, and health sciences education. With these strengths, librarians can easily adapt normal services to meet the community needs after a disaster strikes. Examples of these services follow:

- General support: Librarians can provide a community gathering place, Internet access, mobile units for shelters, emotional support, management and dispersal of donations, and volunteer coordination, and they can help with a variety of tasks, such as finding family members, jobs, and apartments; arranging for prescription medication refills; and locating shelters for animals.

- Children's resources and services: Whether children are stuck at home with no electricity or displaced in a shelter, a public or school library can offer access to books, resources, and programming to keep children entertained during a stressful time. These services can be offered in the library, if it is open, or in other public facilities or shelters. Making services available off-site allows staff to work even if the library is closed because of lack of utilities or damage.
- Information community builders: In the past, librarians have been involved in mass book donation projects, provided restoration support to damaged sister libraries, shared information through interlibrary loan, promoted preparedness activities, housed displaced information professionals, and established buddy systems for libraries to ensure continued services for communities.

Educators and Trainers

Whether one-on-one or in a classroom setting, most librarians provide training on some level whenever they assist clients. Because teaching in a variety of settings is integral to the profession, librarians can easily step in and train victims, first responders, and others throughout the preparedness, response, and recovery cycle.

- Train the trainer: Before a disaster strikes, librarians can train first responders to use valuable resources, especially the free resources like WISER (Wireless Information System for Emergency Responders) from the National Library of Medicine. Being trained before something happens will allow first responders to utilize new skills and knowledge while also sharing their experience with colleagues.
- Post-event training: After an event, both those affected by the disaster and those responding to it need quick access to information. Librarians can provide the training and the conduit to connect diverse groups of users with the information they need. In addition to working one-on-one with victims, librarians can go to shelters and teach classes on how to find timely, relevant information concerning insurance, other shelter locations, assistance with food/housing, as well as details about FEMA programs and other services.

Nontraditional Roles

During a large-scale disaster the library will be closed in many instances; however, services do not have to be curtailed. As discussed in chapter 3, the library's electronic resources are typically available 24/7 even though the library itself is closed. Services may also be maintained through remote access. Additional opportunities for librarians to be involved in more non-traditional ways include volunteering for the local Community Emergency Response Team (CERT), completing the National Incident Management System (NIMS) Incident Command System (ICS) training, and volunteering in a Joint Information Center (JIC) during an actual event.

Community Emergency Response Teams

The CERT program informs laypeople about disaster preparedness for hazards that may impact their area and trains them in basic disaster response skills such as fire safety, light search and rescue, team organization, and disaster medical operations (http://www.citzencorps.fema.gov/cert/). By applying concepts learned in the classroom and during exercises, CERT members are prepared to assist others with response efforts in their neighborhood or workplace when professional responders are not immediately available. CERT members are also encouraged to support emergency response agencies by assuming a more active role in emergency preparedness projects in the community.

The CERT concept was developed and implemented by the City of Los Angeles Fire Department to address the need for trained civilians when responding to earthquakes. The training furthers citizens' understanding of their responsibility in preparing for disaster and increases their ability to safely assist community members following an event. CERT programs help communities supplement response capability and capacity after a disaster, enabling quicker response and fewer casualties.

CERT training is provided by first responders who have the requisite knowledge and skills to instruct the sessions. The training consists of seven sessions covering such topics as disaster preparedness, fire suppression, basic medical operations, search and rescue, disaster psychology, and team organization. CERT is about readiness, with the fundamental tenets of people helping people, rescuer safety, and doing the greatest good for the community. CERT is a positive and realistic approach to emergency and disaster situations, recognizing that citizens will initially be on their own and that their actions can make a difference. Through training, citizens can manage utilities and put out small fires; avoid three causes of death by opening airways, controlling bleeding, and treating for shock; provide basic medical aid; search for and rescue victims safely; and organize themselves and other volunteers into an effective workforce.

So, you ask, why would a librarian find it important to be trained as a CERT volunteer? There are many reasons.

- The library, as a resource provider, is always considered an integral part of a "community," with community being defined as a town, corporation, school, university, hospital, and so forth. In the event of a disaster, a librarian will be even more valuable to the team if trained to respond to events that will help the community plan, respond, and recover. An example of a role the librarian could play would be to assist the community in creating a disaster plan. Or, the librarian can assist with recovery after a disaster if properly trained in search and recovery and basic medical skills.

- A CERT-trained librarian can participate in community activities that affect an area but might not have direct impact on the library. For example, in April 2010, the Escambia County CERT in Florida assisted in the management of volunteer cleanup aimed at removing debris from beaches in Pensacola and Perdido. The goal of the cleanup was to reduce the amount of contaminated material in case any oil from the Deep Water Horizon disaster came on shore. In March 2010, another example involved CERT volunteers in Cameron, Missouri, who helped the local sheriff's department successfully search for an 82-year-old woman who had been missing for over 24 hours.

- When embedded in a CERT, it is easier for a librarian to offer training to other CERT volunteers and staff. In Brazoria County, Texas, an active CERT volunteer, who is also a medical librarian, applied to the National Network of Libraries of Medicine South Central Region for funding to train local first responders to search the WISER database made available by the National Library of Medicine. These classes were structured with a train-the-trainer model in mind so that first responders attending the initial sessions could deliver future classes to other colleagues and citizens (Halsted, internal communication).

Benefits of CERT Training

In 2005, the year Hurricane Katrina struck, I was the Associate Director of the National Network of Libraries of Medicine South Central Region. While attempting to assist network members in the New Orleans area, I quickly realized that I was unaware of the emergency response infrastructure and how decisions were made that affected individuals, in both their personal and work lives. Encouraged by a coworker, I enrolled in CERT with the goals of learning about the emergency response infrastructure and how librarians might be able to position the library, within a community, before an emergency occurs.

CERT made me aware of the roles and relationships among national, state, county, and city emergency response agencies and how and when the agencies are activated. In addition to learning basic disaster response skills, I gained insight into the general needs and priorities during emergencies as well as potential emergency response groups librarians could target with health information outreach efforts.

−Renée Bougard
Outreach Librarian
National Library of Medicine
Bethesda, MD

National Incident Management System Incident Command System

The National Incident Management System (NIMS) is an emergency response system that is designed to improve preparation, coordination, and incident management in the event of a crisis (http://www.nimsonline .com/incident-command/incident-command-system) by bringing together disaster response personnel at the federal, state, and local agency levels. NIMS was developed and implemented after the 2001 terrorist attacks at the World Trade Center and the Pentagon.

In 2004 the Incident Command System (ICS) was incorporated into NIMS following California wildfires that caused massive property damage and resulted in fatalities. Studies conducted after the disaster showed that management and communication deficiencies were primarily to blame for the loss of life and property rather than lack of resources or ineffective tactics.

ICS is a protocol detailing how personnel, policies, procedures, facilities, resources, and equipment all work together in an organized structure to respond to an emergency or prevent a crisis from happening. ICS established many key concepts that serve as a foundation for proper emergency response in the event of a crisis:

- Unity of command: In an emergency response situation, every person working on a task reports to only one supervisor. This rule eliminates the possibility of individuals receiving conflicting information and orders from a variety of supervisors and suppresses potential confusion that can happen in a chain of command. Unity of command also increases accountability, prevents freelancing, facilitates the flow of information, better coordinates operations, and ensures safety of all workers in the emergency situation.
- Universal terminology: Before the establishment of ICS, agencies developed and used unique terminology for their operations. Consequently, a term used in one agency may mean something completely different in another. When agencies are required to work together during an emergency the potential for confusion among personnel is elevated if a common vocabulary is not used. ICS promotes and requires the use of a universal terminology, and a bank of terms has been developed to apply a consistent meaning to words.
- Management by objective: In ICS, this concept means that a task is not assigned until a clear objective is established that the task will help accomplish. Objectives should be specific, attainable, and accompanied by a precise time frame for completion.
- Flexible and modular organization: Organizations and individuals who are needed at a current point in time are utilized and then dismissed immediately after their duties are completed. This strategy helps minimize costs and improves efficiency.

Special Skills Training

Want to learn more? Or, just want to find out if Citizen Corps is for you? We will be hosting a series of trainings each month around the county where we will provide training on new topics and reviewing skills learned in CERT and MRC core trainings.

We're starting this month with training on hazardous materials. Learn more about toxic chemicals commonly found in our area and how to identify them and protect your family if you are involved in a chemical emergency.

This is hands-on training with web-based tools that are free from the National Library of Medicine.

We will be presenting this training February 21st from 6:30–8:30 p.m. at the Alvin Senior Center, 309 W. Sealey in Alvin.

Everyone is welcome. Stay tuned to find out when we will be in your area.

(Training Notice from the Brazoria County, Texas, CERT Program)

- Span-of-control: Any given individual's span of control should be between three and seven people. A manager should not be spread too thin by being made responsible for too many subordinates. If more than seven individuals are supervised by one person, the manager's workload may become too great.

Basic ICS training is easy and can be done online at the Emergency Management Institute's website. More advanced courses, such as ICS-300: Intermediate ICS for Expanding Incidents, must be taken in a classroom setting since participation in disaster scenarios and prior knowledge of the command structure and terminology are required (Federal Emergency Management Agency, 2011). These classes are taught regionally by instructors certified by FEMA.

Many areas of ICS are a good fit for the skills and talents of librarians. First is that of Incident Command, in the event that the disaster is centrally located in or near the library. Training in ICS will allow the library director or designate to set up a command structure for recovery efforts. With the proper training, the library's COOP plan can be based on the ICS structure, designating key staff for specific roles. Planning also allows for identification of backup personnel in the event that key staff members are not available.

There are two other underlying benefits to ICS training. First, with the training, librarians become familiar with the common command structure and terminology. In the event of a disaster, the librarian will be seen as more of a partner in recovery efforts if he or she can "walk the walk and talk the talk" of other first responders. Additionally, ICS training provides expertise in completing the FEMA forms that are required to receive recovery funding from that agency.

Benefits of ICS Training

Soon after the tragic events of September 11, 2001 (which closely followed widespread flooding in Houston, Texas, caused by Tropical Storm Allison), the Texas Medical Center (TMC) invited representatives from member institutions to become involved in campus-wide disaster planning efforts. These efforts included NIMS ICS training. Since I had already become involved with my local county CERT team and had personally been trained in the basic ICS courses, I volunteered for the TMC Library planning efforts. At first, the person who headed the TMC disaster planning teams seemed to think, "Okay, Ms. Librarian, you can work with us, but we are not sure what role you would play in a real disaster." As I continued to volunteer for committee assignments and duties, the TMC community came to realize that librarians can play critical roles. We excel in information gathering and dissemination, program management, and communications. After about a year, I found that I was cochairing planning committees. I was invited to the intense, three-day ICS-300 training, where I learned many valuable skills applicable to a disaster in the library or a more widespread event. I feel that participation in ICS training has elevated the image of the library in our own local community.

−Deborah Halsted, MLS, MA
Houston Academy of Medicine-Texas Medical Center Library
Houston, TX

JIC Drill Skills

I participated in a Joint Information Center drill in Houston, Texas, in 2007. I came equipped with my small netbook computer, a broadband card for connectivity, and enthusiasm. During the drill I was able to quickly download information and give it directly to the people who needed it most by taking my small computer to them. Other participants were using shared computers and writing up notes on large flip charts in various areas of the room. After the drill, a representative from the U.S. Coast Guard commended me on my information gathering and dissemination skills. I told him that was what librarians do on a daily basis and that it just came naturally. To me, it was a perfect fit for a librarian.

–Deborah Halsted, MLS, MA
Houston Academy of Medicine-Texas Medical Center Library
Houston, TX

National Incident Management System Joint Information System

Public information consists of the processes, procedures, and systems to communicate timely, accurate, and accessible information on the incident's cause, size, and current situation to the public, responders, and additional stakeholders, both directly and indirectly affected (http://www.fema.gov/emergency/nims/Publicinformation.shtm). Public information must be coordinated and integrated across jurisdictions and organizations involved in the incident to include, federal, state, tribal, and local governments; private sector entities; and nongovernmental organizations. To facilitate that process, public information includes three major systems/components: Public Information Officers (PIOs), the Joint Information System (JIS), and the Joint Information Center (JIC).

A JIS provides the mechanism to organize, integrate, and coordinate information to ensure timely, accurate, accessible, and consistent messaging across multiple jurisdictions and/or disciplines with nongovernmental organizations and the private sector. A JIS includes the plans, protocols, procedures, and structures used to provide public information. A JIC is a central location that facilitates operation of the JIS. The JIC is where personnel with public information responsibilities perform critical emergency information functions, crisis communications, and public affairs functions. JICs may be established at various levels of government or at incident sites or may be components of Multiagency Coordination Systems. A single JIC location is preferable, but the system is flexible and adaptable enough to accommodate virtual or multiple JIC locations, as required.

Because a major part of a JIC is information gathering and dissemination, this is a perfect niche for a librarian to fill, provided service disruptions in the library itself are not overwhelming. Additionally, JIC training gives librarians insight into working with the media, which can be a challenge in the best of situations and emphasizes the importance of appointing designated spokespeople to minimize the dissemination of inaccurate or proprietary information.

Conclusion

This chapter provided suggestions about the many roles librarians can play in preparedness, recovery, and response. While some of the roles described represent traditional activities, others, such as getting involved with CERT, may force librarians out of their comfort zones. Special training, such as the NIMS ICS training, can inspire librarians to take on new roles, equipping them with the tools they need to hit the ground running. Regardless of whether the library is providing traditional or nontraditional services, or more likely a combination of the two, following a crisis, a disaster ultimately offers librarians a chance to "think outside the box" and establish a new realm of service and support.

References

American Library Association (ALA). 2011. "ALA Commends Sen. Reed for Efforts to Ensure FEMA Provision Includes Libraries as Temporary Relocation Facilities." ALA. http://connect.ala.org/node/127510.

Featherstone, Robin M., Becky J. Lyon, and Angela B. Ruffin. 2008. "Library Roles in Disaster Response: An Oral History Project by the National Library of Medicine." *Journal of the Medical Library Association* 96, no. 4: 343–350.

Federal Emergency Management Agency (FEMA). 2011. *NIMS Training Program.* FEMA. http://www.fema.gov/emergency/nims/NIMSTrainingCourses.shtm.

Zach, Lisl, and Michelynn McKnight. 2010. "Innovative Service Improvised During Disasters: Evidence-Based Education Modules to Prepare Students and Practitioners for Shifts in Community Information Needs." *Journal of Education for Library and Information Science* 51, no. 2: 76–85.

Two Model Scenarios for Cooperative Engagement

8

Do you want to know who you are? Don't ask. Act! Action will delineate and define you.

—Thomas Jefferson

While there are many types of disasters, two basic categories that each fits into are those which allow time to prepare and those which strike without notice. Hurricanes fall into the first category because, under normal circumstances, modern technology allows for a few days to prepare, whether this means boarding up home and business or evacuating with the family. On the other hand, there is virtually no warning for an earthquake beyond knowing that you live in an earthquake-prone area, requiring you to be constantly on guard.

This chapter offers two fictional scenarios, one of how a library can plan for and respond to a hurricane and one, on the other end of the scale, where a library can respond to a sudden natural disaster, in this case an earthquake. It should be stressed again to conduct regular risk assessments as described in chapter 1 so that all library staff are aware of potential threats and have made plans on how to respond to particular disasters.

As you read through these scenarios, keep in mind that they represent disasters that you can prepare for and disasters that allow no time for preparation. Therefore, in your planning you can substitute a hurricane with other service disruptions that offer advanced warning, such as a severe winter storm or even a lengthy closure due to renovation. In place of earthquakes, you can substitute a tornado or a shooter. Finally, interspersed within these fictional stories are actual resources that you can use for your disaster planning activities.

IN THIS CHAPTER:

✓ Hurricane Jenny

✓ The Marshall City Earthquake

✓ Conclusion

✓ References

A 10-Step Approach to Service Continuity Planning

Step 1: Assess risks

Step 2: Protect yourself, your staff, and your patrons

Step 3: Create procedures to ensure continuation of core services

Step 4: Create procedures to ensure access to core materials

Step 5: Develop a Mutual Aid Agreement with another library or network

Step 6: Proactively plan for the rescue and recovery of your highly valued materials

Step 7: Develop a communication plan

Step 8: Know how to obtain outside assistance

Step 9: Develop a PReP for Service Continuity

Step 10: Be prepared at home

(Wilson, 2012b)

Hurricane Jenny

On September 8, Hurricane Jenny was located just north of Hispania and tracking to the northwest. Her winds were approaching 120 miles per hour, a Category 3 storm. Hurricane watches were activated along the eastern seaboard from Miami to Savannah.

In Kingsville, Georgia, a town of a little more than 20,000 people and located 40 miles inland and about 70 miles south of Savannah, Royal County emergency officials, headed by Keith Bickers, were meeting to discuss the potential impact of the storm, which was still at least three days away. Down the street at the Kingsville Public Library, Maggie Carson, library director, was also keeping a watchful eye on the storm by monitoring national weather sites and Twitter.

In June, Maggie had had a lunch meeting with Keith at the Kingsville Diner, where they discussed possible roles that Kingsville Public Library staff could play in an emergency. Maggie shared with Keith an article by Rebecca Hamilton titled "State Library of Louisiana and Public Libraries' Response to Hurricanes: Lessons, Issues and Strategies" (Hamilton, 2011). Maggie highlighted the section of the document that listed roles public libraries played following Hurricane Katrina that Hamilton had pulled from two published articles (Dickerson, 2006; Cosper-LeBoeuf, 2006). She showed Keith how libraries increased their hours and visited shelters with books and magazines in order to improve morale and give the evacuees a sense of normalcy. In addition, library meeting rooms were turned into computer rooms so evacuees and out-of-state workers could check e-mail, locate family members, file for insurance, and fill out FEMA (Federal Emergency Management Agency) forms.

Keith particularly liked the idea of using the library as a place of normalcy, and he told her that he'd look into the possibility of using mobile backup generators to power laptops and other devices should the library lose power. However, he cautioned Maggie that if the public library was going to commit to this role, then he needed to be certain that Maggie would have staff available to open and close the library. Maggie agreed. Before their meeting ended they also decided to designate the library as a backup command center should their primary location at City Hall go down.

Maggie understood the gravity of her library's new role, and she met with her staff a day later to discuss strategy. Kingsville Public Library has three full-time staff: Maggie, the director; Dan Carpenter, head of Public Services; and Maya Thill, head of Collection Management. Dan and Maya agreed to help staff the library should a major disaster strike Kingsville. Dan, a father of three, did state that although he was committed to staff the library, his family's needs would come first. The library also has two part-time employees and several volunteers; all offered their assistance, if needed.

Excitedly, Maggie called Keith to say that her staff was on board. Keith listened and expressed great appreciation for their service. Since Dan expressed concern about his family, Keith suggested that Maggie call their local chapter of the American Red Cross to get training on how to be prepared for a disaster at home. He also suggested that she distribute the Red Cross's Hurricane Safety Checklist to her staff, since hurricanes were their highest risk.

Maggie had become interested in emergency preparedness at a May conference she attended at the Georgia University Medical School (GUMS) Health Sciences Library. The conference featured speakers, breakout sessions, and a workshop on the importance of libraries keeping their core services and resources available following a disaster. The keynote speaker, a person from the South Carolina Department of Health and Environmental Control, spoke about the importance of consumer health information following a disaster and encouraged participants to partner with Public Health on ways to improve the availability of consumer health following a disaster.

The last speaker of the morning was a member of the Southeastern/Atlantic Region (SE/A) of the National Network of Libraries of Medicine (NN/LM) who spoke of funding opportunities for libraries to partner with local emergency planners and community agencies. Following the NN/LM speaker, Maggie met Carrie Jamison, a librarian at the GUMS library, who was very knowledgeable about emergency preparedness and response and was the coordinator of their emergency response plan. They agreed to work together on developing a proposal to partner the Kingsville Public Library with the Coastal Public Health District for using the library to enhance awareness of health issues following a disaster. Following lunch, participants attended a workshop titled "A 10-Step Approach to Service Continuity Planning" (Wilson, 2012b). In the workshop, participants learned the value of proactively planning for a disaster, including determining risks, ensuring continuity of core resources and services, protecting hard-to-replace or rare materials, being prepared at home, and how to create a one-page service continuity plan. Maggie was particularly impressed with the one-page plan and made it a goal to have one completed within two weeks after the workshop. In addition to completing the one-page plan, she made it a goal to raise the readiness level of her library using the guide "15 Elements Demonstrated by a Library at a High State of Readiness" (Wilson, 2012a).

A week after the conference, Maggie contacted her local chapter of the American Red Cross about home preparedness training. She discovered that the chapter offered a class on demand and would be happy to teach it at the library. Because this information would be of value to the entire community, Maggie promoted it on the library's website and over 25 people attended. The timing of the training turned out to be fortuitous, because less than three months later Hurricane Jenny would challenge the community's disaster preparedness capabilities.

As Hurricane Jenny churned northwestward, watches gradually changed to warnings from Brunswick, Georgia, to Wilmington, North Carolina. Officials in Kingsville, just 60 miles north of Brunswick, ramped up emergency operations and discussed evacuation strategies. The storm was still two days away, but the National Weather Center raised the probability that it would

15 Elements Demonstrated by a Library at a High State of Readiness

1. Comprehensive Disaster Plan updated at least once a year
2. Response station that includes posted response procedures and ready access to tools (e.g., flashlights, first aid kit, bullhorn, plastic, battery-operated radio, etc.) for handling an emergency
3. One-Page Service Continuity Pocket Response Plan (PReP) updated at least quarterly
4. Shelter-in-place location
5. Communication plan that incorporates redundancy of means of communication (such as what to do if cell phones don't work) and procedures for updating website, Facebook page, and/or Twitter
6. Service continuity team
7. At least one scheduled evacuation drill per year
8. At least one tabletop exercise per year
9. Library and/or librarians integrated into parent institution's disaster plan
10. Core print textbooks/materials identified and labeled or shelved together
11. Servers with core online resources on unlimited emergency power
12. Mutual Aid Agreements with other libraries or networks for delivery of core services
13. Prioritized recovery list of all valuable and hard-to-replace materials
14. Partnership (contract not required) with commercial salvage and recovery company (e.g., BELFOR, BMS, Polygon)
15. 72-Hour emergency kits at the homes of all members of service continuity team

(Wilson, 2012a)

What Is a State of Emergency?

"The Governor declares a State of Emergency when he/she believes a disaster has occurred or may be imminent that is severe enough to require State aid to supplement local resources in preventing or alleviating damages, loss, hardship, or suffering. This declaration authorizes the Governor to speed State agency assistance to communities in need. It enables him to make resources immediately available to rescue, evacuate, shelter, provide essential commodities (i.e., heating fuel, food, etc.), and quell disturbances in affected localities. It may also position the State to seek federal assistance when the scope of the event exceeds the State's resources."

(New Jersey Office of Emergency Management, 2012)

make landfall as a Category 3 storm. At the Kingsville Public Library, Maggie, Dan, and Maya met to discuss their communications plan.

Maggie began the meeting by sharing something she heard at the NN/LM workshop: without a communications plan, you might as well not have a plan. She was glad that they had a communications plan in place and had recently tested their primary and backup communication strategies. Maggie, Dan, and Maya's primary communications mode would be a noncordless landline phone because these types of phones are most reliable following a disaster. In the event that the phones were down, the backup plan was texting. If they needed to discuss something as a group, they would use Skype. They also agreed to fill up their car tanks and would have their car chargers available to charge portable devices in the event of power loss.

Maggie checked in with Carrie over at the Georgia University Medical School Health Sciences Library. Carrie reported that their library's Service Continuity Team had just met and that their plan was on standby and would likely be activated by the next morning. Carrie wished Maggie well and offered her assistance, if needed.

Twelve hours before Hurricane Jenny was to make landfall, the National Hurricane Center issued a statement that the storm would hit as either a Category 2 or 3 storm 50 miles south of Kingsville, meaning they would likely suffer from the strongest winds on the right side of its eyewall. Maggie checked the Saffir-Simpson Hurricane Wind Scale and noted that regardless of whether Jenny was Category 2 or 3, large-scale power outages were likely. The governor had issued mandatory evacuation orders for residents along the coast, and Kingsville Red Cross volunteers were opening shelters. All schools and county agencies, including the library, were closed so that everyone could make the necessary preparations. Maggie called Dan and Maya to test their primary communications strategy. She then tested their backup system by sending them a text message. Each test was successful. Before retiring for the night, Maggie put a message on the library's website that the library would be closed until further notice. She put the same announcement on the library's voice messaging system and its Facebook page.

Hurricane Jenny made landfall at 1:14 a.m. on September 11 with sustained winds near 100 mph. A nighttime hurricane can be extremely frightening, and Jenny was no exception. Within 30 minutes of hurricane-force winds, the power flickered twice and then went out over much of Kingsville. The local radio station, WKGV, suspended all syndicated programming and was accepting calls from local residents and releasing bulletins from emergency planning officials. Maggie still had power and was listening to the community reports. The situation did not sound good. At 2:10 a.m. Maggie's lights flickered again and then went out. An eerie quiet surrounded her as the eye of the hurricane moved overhead.

At daylight, the hurricane-force winds had diminished greatly. Residents wandered outside and were met by downed tree limbs and power lines. Power was out everywhere. At 9:00 a.m. Maggie called Dan and Maya. Both were safe. Since everyone was without electricity, Maggie realized that there was little that they could do from home, and she told Dan and Maya that they would most likely not be needed until power was restored.

Soon after Maggie talked with her staff, Keith called and reported that a large live oak tree was hanging precariously over their office. He asked if they could set up their mobile command center in the library's parking lot. Maggie readily agreed, realizing that a mobile command center in the parking lot would demonstrate how the library can be part of the town's recovery effort.

The day turned into night and power was still out all over town. Maggie had not opened her refrigerator at all and was wondering about the storage life of some of the food. In particular, she was concerned about the meat she had purchased two days ago. The Kingsville CERT (Citizen Emergency Response Team) was operating a help line for nonemergency calls, so Maggie dialed the number, 946-INFO. The person who answered sounded familiar, and Maggie asked if it was Diane, one of her two volunteers. It was, and Diane explained that she had gone through the eight-week CERT training and specialized in public information. Maggie asked about meat spoilage, and Diane read from a pamphlet from the U.S. Department of Agriculture.

Since it had been more than four hours since the power was off, Maggie tossed the meat in her trash. She ate a cheese sandwich and a salad, then lit her kerosene lantern and settled in for the evening.

A spectacular sun rose the next morning and power was still out across town. Maggie noted from talking to her neighbors that a sense of anxiety was settling over the town. All pharmacies in town were closed, as were the grocery stores. People in need of prescriptions were especially nervous.

Maggie's phone rang; it was Keith. He was at the mobile command center and asked if Maggie would be willing to join him and discuss some recovery strategies. Maggie readily agreed and took off on foot to the library. Along her way, she was astonished by the damage. Tree limbs were down everywhere and people were out picking up branches and sharing "war" stories with neighbors. The undulating sounds of chainsaws followed her as she walked along.

When Maggie arrived at the command center, Keith showed her around. In the trailer were operational computers, each powered from an emergency generator. In addition to the computers, Keith had access to other types of communication, so he was apprised of the situation and knew that the likely time for power to be restored to 50 percent of the town would not be until the next morning. Maggie was introduced to a FEMA worker who was in charge of the relief effort. He asked Maggie if it would be possible to set up a disaster relief center at the library for residents to fill out forms and get information. Maggie agreed and then went inside the library with Keith and the FEMA worker to find the best available site. She chose the community room, as this was near the entrance, and asked Keith about power. He told her that the library was a priority location and that library power should be restored by midafternoon. Keith then asked Maggie a big favor: because the community has been under a lot of stress, he asked if it would be possible

Keeping Food Safe During an Emergency

Did you know that a flood, fire, national disaster, or the loss of power from high winds, snow, or ice could jeopardize the safety of your food? Knowing how to determine if food is safe and how to keep food safe will help minimize the potential loss of food and reduce the risk of foodborne illness. This fact sheet will help you make the right decisions for keeping your family safe during an emergency.

ABCD's of Keeping Food Safe in an Emergency

Always keep meat, poultry, fish, and eggs refrigerated at or below 40°F and frozen food at or below 0°F. This may be difficult when the power is out.

Keep the refrigerator and freezer doors closed as much as possible to maintain the cold temperature. The refrigerator will keep food safely cold for about 4 hours if it is unopened. A full freezer will hold the temperature for approximately 48 hours (24 hours if it is half full) if the door remains closed. Obtain dry or block ice to keep your refrigerator as cold as possible if the power is going to be out for a prolonged period of time. Fifty pounds of dry ice should hold an 18-cubic-foot full freezer for 2 days. Plan ahead and know where dry ice and block ice can be purchased.

(Reprinted from U.S. Department of Agriculture Food Safety and Inspection Service, 2013)

During an Earthquake

Drop, Cover, and Hold On. Minimize your movements to a few steps to a nearby safe place, and if you are indoors, stay there until the shaking has stopped and you are sure exiting is safe.

If Indoors

- DROP to the ground; take COVER by getting under a sturdy table or other piece of furniture; and HOLD ON until the shaking stops. If there isn't a table or desk near you, cover your face and head with your arms and crouch in an inside corner of the building.
- Stay away from glass, windows, outside doors and walls, and anything that could fall, such as lighting fixtures or furniture.
- Stay in bed if you are there when the earthquake strikes. Hold on and protect your head with a pillow, unless you are under a heavy light fixture that could fall. In that case, move to the nearest safe place.
- Do not use a doorway except if you know it is a strongly supported, load-bearing doorway and it is close to you. Many inside doorways are lightly constructed and do not offer protection.
- Stay inside until the shaking stops and it is safe to go outside. Do not exit a building during the shaking. Research has shown that most injuries occur when people inside buildings attempt to move to a different location inside the building or try to leave.
- DO NOT use the elevators.
- Be aware that the electricity may go out or the sprinkler systems or fire alarms may turn on.

Continued on p. 109

for her to open up the entire library for at least a couple of hours tomorrow. Maggie was thrilled at the opportunity and offered to keep it open as late as was needed. She posted a sign on the door that the library would be open tomorrow and contacted the local radio station. She even called Diane at the CERT help line and asked her to pass along the news to callers.

The next morning, Maggie showed up at the library at seven o'clock. With electricity restored at the library and with pockets of power available elsewhere, she put a notice on the library's website of the open hours and of the library's temporary status as the town's disaster relief site. Dan arrived about an hour later and Maya followed soon after. At nine o'clock they opened the library to a group of very thankful people. The children rushed over to the children's section, and many of the adults headed to the computers, new books, and DVDs. The remainder followed the signs to the FEMA disaster relief center and began filling out forms, reading e-mail, and locating family members.

A steady stream of residents came through the library all day, including the mayor of Kingsville, who said she had power but wanted to be where all the action was. She personally thanked Maggie, Dan, and Maya and then headed over to the children's section where her two children were pouring through anime. With pride, Maggie looked around the room and thought, "This is what service to the community is all about."

The Marshall City Earthquake

From her seat on the train, Kelly Tyson marveled at the beauty of the morning. Far off in the east, the peaks of the Sierra Nevada Mountains were silhouetted against the early morning sun, the tallest peaks still covered with snow. As the train slowed, she watched as a flock of turkey vultures circled upward and downward, as if caught in the vortex of a tornado, above the carcass of some animal hidden in a thicket, out of her sight. Her reverie was interrupted by the announcement of her station, Marshall City. The doors opened and she and a bevy of commuters scrambled off the train, forming a river of humanity heading through the station gate, some walking to work, and some searching for a cab or a city bus. Kelly headed to the hospital.

Kelly is the librarian at the Marshall City Regional Hospital (MCRH), a not-for-profit hospital not far from Oakland, California. She has worked at MCRH for 23 years. The library, currently located on the ground floor of the hospital, has moved three times in the past ten years. With each move the library gets smaller and moves farther away from the original location near the hospital lobby.

Kelly always arrives early. Her day always starts with a cup of chai that she sips on while spending her first hour answering e-mail messages and catching up on her RSS feeds. She read her first message, which was from Hannah Michaels, MCRH Director of Emergency Preparedness. Hannah's message contained the minutes from last week's quarterly MCRH Emergency Preparedness and Response Committee meeting. Kelly smiled as she looked through the minutes and felt proud about the many times that she and the library were mentioned.

Kelly liked working with Hannah, who recognized the value of the library in the event of a disaster. They both worked on a number of grants, including an award from the NN/LM Pacific Southwest Region for an iPad project that included the procurement of five iPads loaded with clinical care apps that would be distributed, where needed, following a disaster. Kelly and Hannah also worked out a plan in which the library would be used as a crisis center in the result of an incident with multiple casualties. To facilitate this arrangement, Hannah secured funding for the installation of emergency power outlets in the library.

It was nice having emergency power at the library, but Kelly knew that in the event of a major disaster print materials might still be needed if temporary clinical areas had to be set up where power and the Internet were not available. On a book truck near her office, she had multiple copies of textbooks identified as essential by readers of the National Library of Medicine's Disaster Information Management Research Center's (DIMRC) disaster outreach electronic discussion list (Wilson, 2011), including these:

> *Current Emergency Diagnosis and Treatment*
> *Emergency Medicine: A Comprehensive Study Guide*
> *The 5-Minute Clinical Consult*
> *Goldfrank's Toxicologic Emergencies*
> *Gray's Anatomy*
> *Harrison's Principles of Internal Medicine*
> *Mandell, Douglas, and Bennett's Principles and Practices of Infectious Diseases*
> *The Merck Manual of Diagnosis and Therapy*
> *Nelson's Textbook of Pediatrics*
> *Physicians' Desk Reference*
> *Rosen's Emergency Medicine: Concepts and Clinical Practice*

Kelly's office is located near the library's service desk where she can easily provide backup support. Her office is filled with recognition plaques and prints of northern New Mexico, where she spends two weeks in June at a bed and breakfast in Taos. Her desk, ever neat and tidy, juts out perpendicularly from the wall. Florescent lights provide light from the drop-down tiled ceiling.

Just as Kelly had finished her drink and was about to head out to wish her staff a good morning, the building started to shake. Kelly grabbed hold of her desk while her mind frantically tried to make sense of the situation. Was it an explosion? A train wreck? Did a plane hit the building? As the building continued to shake, she remembered the earthquake drill that took place

Continued from p. 108

If Outdoors

- Stay there.
- Move away from buildings, streetlights, and utility wires.
- Once in the open, stay there until the shaking stops. The greatest danger exists directly outside buildings, at exits and alongside exterior walls. Many of the 120 fatalities from the 1933 Long Beach earthquake occurred when people ran outside of buildings only to be killed by falling debris from collapsing walls. Ground movement during an earthquake is seldom the direct cause of death or injury. Most earthquake-related casualties result from collapsing walls, flying glass, and falling objects.

If in a Moving Vehicle

- Stop as quickly as safety permits and stay in the vehicle. Avoid stopping near or under buildings, trees, overpasses, and utility wires.
- Proceed cautiously once the earthquake has stopped. Avoid roads, bridges, or ramps that might have been damaged by the earthquake.

If Trapped Under Debris

- Do not light a match.
- Do not move about or kick up dust.
- Cover your mouth with a handkerchief or clothing.
- Tap on a pipe or wall so rescuers can locate you. Use a whistle if one is available. Shout only as a last resort. Shouting can cause you to inhale dangerous amounts of dust.

(Reprinted from Federal Emergency Management Agency, 2012)

How Psychologists Help in a Crisis

As psychologists offer this support, they may:

- Listen to people's concerns on a variety of issues, including their homes, missing family members, and pets.
- Help people to manage their temporary living conditions and to acclimate to shelters located possibly far from their home state and in different environments.
- Provide information about available resources for current needs (clothing, medical care, etc.); help to facilitate those connections.
- Advocate for the needs of particular individuals or families as they navigate the systems that have been established to provide aid.
- Help individuals to develop resilience skills by making connections with family and friends who've also survived; accepting that change is going to be an ongoing experience; maintaining a hopeful outlook; and helping people to develop their own personal recovery plans.
- Listen to parents' concerns about how their children will recover from the disaster and manage potential challenges ahead (e.g., new schools, etc.).

Continued on p. 111

a month ago, so she DROPPED to the floor, COVERED herself under her desk, and HELD ON. The shaking seemed to last forever. While Kelly was under her desk, she could see the legs and shoes of some fellow employees as they ran by her office in a state of panic. She could also hear shouts from unfamiliar voices, library patrons, out in the lobby.

When the shaking stopped, Kelly crawled out from under the desk and looked around her office. Some of the prints had fallen off their hooks and were on the floor; a tile had fallen from the ceiling and smashed on the floor; and a lighting fixture hung precariously near her door. Power was still on.

As Kelly emerged from her office, she surveyed the lobby and noticed some damage. Two large portraits of former doctors were askew, and several ceiling tiles and light fixtures were on the floor. Kelly was alone in the library; her staff and patrons had vacated the building in the first wave of evacuees.

Kelly used her cell phone to call home to check on her family. The call did not go through, and she remembered that there is a good chance that cell phones would not work following an unexpected event as the volume of calls overloads the system, so she used the desk phone to make a quick call home and texted her daughter at University of California, Los Angeles. Everyone was shaken up, but fine. Kelly's daughter reported that it was a 6.9-magnitude earthquake and the epicenter was about two miles east of Marshall City.

As Kelly started to leave the library to see if there was any damage outside, the power went out. She walked out and joined the staff and patrons who were waiting for advice from the Emergency Preparedness Office. Instead of advice, Kelly got a text from Hannah telling her that there were multiple casualties coming in from two tour buses that crashed when a bridge broke off its supports 10 miles northeast of Marshall City. Hannah, currently at the emergency room, would be at the library shortly to set up a crisis center for noninjured passengers and family members of those who sustained injuries. Because time was short, Hannah dispatched an aid to the library to give Kelly a quick overview of the role psychologists play in a crisis. Kelly agreed to function in the role of providing resource assistance.

When Hannah arrived, they prepared the classroom by arranging desks and plugging laptops into the emergency power outlets. Hannah thanked Kelly for her assistance and said that crisis center staff would be showing up to fine-tune their setup. Kelly reminded Hannah of the print core textbook collection that was available, if needed, and offered to bring the print text-book collection into the classroom and to be available to answer questions from health-care professionals. As Hannah left the room, she smiled and said that she would announce her availability to everyone in the ER and at auxiliary clinics. Kelly rolled the textbooks into the classroom, found a spot near the back of the room, and plugged in her laptop. She was ready.

Within the next 60 minutes, family members of the injured tourists began arriving, most still visibly upset. Crisis Center personnel administered counseling while Kelly directed others to computers and offered assistance retrieving any kind of information. As more people arrived, Kelly directed them to the browsing section of the library, which had current medical journals as well as a few popular magazines.

Hannah called and said that one of the hospital's clinics that was being used to treat wounded from another mass casualty situation reported a power outage and needed any kind of print textbook, preferably *Harrison's Principles of Internal Medicine*, *Physicians' Desk Reference*, and *The Merck Manual of Diagnosis and Therapy*. She asked Kelly if she could box up either of these texts and be ready for a courier, who was on his way. Kelly, antici-pating this kind of need, had purchased extra copies of these titles and so was able to keep her shelf of print textbooks intact.

By late afternoon, most people had been placed in local hotels. Those people who remained had family members who were critically injured, either in surgery or in the ICU. By 5:30 p.m. Kelly and two staff from the Crisis Center were alone in the library. Hannah thanked Kelly for all her efforts and said that it would be fine to close the library.

All trains were shut down for track inspection, but Kelly was able to secure a ride home from an administrative assistant in Radiology. Many hospital employees were stranded or working overtime to accommodate the influx of patients. As Kelly was leaving she called Hannah and left a message that she could make the library available to staff overnight.

As Kelly watched the evening news, she reflected on how her staff responded to the earthquake by fleeing the building. She made it a point to perform more regular disaster drills, and she searched the Internet to find information on disaster psychology. Finally, she jotted down ideas for keeping a positive morale over the next few weeks while keeping an eye on any behavioral changes in her staff.

Continued from p. 110

- Help problem-solve conflicts among shelter residents; among family members; and among vol-unteers and staff.
- Help people to manage other life disasters that might be happening at the same time (e.g., death or illness of a relative not related to the current event).
- Educate people that it is normal for disaster survivors to have an array of common reactions. Some of these include fears, memories, nightmares, irritable and/or with-drawn emotions, and confusion.
- Assure people that it is possible to recover from disaster and to build fulfilling and satisfying lives.
- In working with children: notice and support positive coping strategies; help children to rees-tablish connections with others; help children to find ways to help others; help families reestablish familiar routines and structures; remind children and families of the importance of taking breaks from recovery efforts and pro-mote healthy self-care.
- Provide information on how and where to seek longer term as-sistance.

(Reprinted from American Psychological Association, 2011)

Continued on p. 113

Conclusion

These two scenarios are designed to illustrate how librarians and libraries can play a major role in preparedness, response, and recovery, and that emergency planning professionals are receptive to partnerships. Taking action will have a ripple effect in your community and beyond. For example, following a recent Emergency Preparedness and Response event designed to develop partnerships among librarians and emergency planners, three librarians went through Medical Reserve Corps (MRC) training. They are now MRC first responders and therefore in position to influence the understanding of the value of librarians before, during, and after a disaster. As more librarians take part in all aspects of emergency planning and response, the greater our value will become to our communities and to the many agencies and politicians charged with protecting the welfare of their constituents.

References

American Psychological Association (APA). 2011. "What Do Psychologists Do at Disaster Sites?" APA. Last updated April. http://www.apa.org/helpcenter/disaster-site.aspx.

———. 2013. "Managing Traumatic Stress: Tips for Recovering from Disasters and Other Traumatic Events." APA. Last revised August. http://www.apa.org/helpcenter/recovering-disasters.aspx.

Cosper-LeBoeuf, Mary. 2006. "Ill Winds: Hurricanes and Public Libraries Along the Gulf Coast." *Public Libraries* 45, no. 3: 58–63.

Dickerson, Lon. 2006. "Building from Disaster: Lessons from Hurricane Katrina." *Alki: The Washington Library Association Journal* 22, no. 1: 16.

Federal Emergency Management Agency (FEMA). 2012. "During an Earthquake." FEMA. http://www.ready.gov/earthquakes.

Hamilton, Rebecca. 2011. "State Library of Louisiana and Public Libraries' Response to Hurricanes: Lessons, Issues and Strategies." *Public Library Quarterly* 30: 40–53. http://www.tandfonline.com/doi/abs/10.1080/01616846.2010.525385#preview.

New Jersey Office of Emergency Management (NJOEM). 2012. "Guide to Hurricane Preparedness: Frequently Asked Questions Regarding a State of Emergency in New Jersey." NJOEM. http://www.nj.gov/njoem/soe_faq.html.

Texas Department of State Health Services (DSHS). 2012. "Public Health Surveillance Tools—Hurricanes." Texas DSHS. Last updated January 10. http://www.dshs.state.tx.us/commprep/disasterepi/surveillance .aspx.

U.S. Department of Agriculture Food Safety and Inspection Service (USDA FSIS). 2013. "Emergency Preparedness: Keeping Food Safe During an Emergency." USDA FSIS. Last modified July 30. http://www.fsis.usda.gov/wps/portal/fsis/topics/food-safety- education/get-answers/food-safety-fact-sheets/emergency- preparedness/keeping-food-safe-during-an-emergency/CT_Index.

Wilson, Daniel T. 2011. "One-Shelf Disaster Library (List of Titles)." National Network of Libraries of Medicine (NN/LM). March 31. http://nnlm.gov/ep/2011/03/31/one-shelf-disaster-library-list- of-titles/.

———. 2012a. "15 Elements Demonstrated by a Library at a High State of Readiness." National Network of Libraries of Medicine (NN/LM). http://nnlm.gov/ep/highest-state-of-library-readiness/ (page discontinued); modified version available: http://nnlm.gov/ ep/2013/12/05/how-ready-is-your-library/.

———. 2012b. "A 10-Step Approach to Service Continuity Planning." National Network of Libraries of Medicine (NN/LM). http://nnlm.gov/ep/10-stepsservice-continuity/.

Continued from p. 112

Thoughts and behavior patterns are affected by the trauma. You might have repeated and vivid memories of the event. These flashbacks may occur for no apparent reason and may lead to physical reactions such as rapid heartbeat or sweating. You may find it difficult to concentrate or make decisions or become more easily confused. Sleep and eating patterns also may be disrupted. Recurring emotional reactions are common. Anniversaries of the event, such as at one month or one year, can trigger upsetting memories of the traumatic experience. These "triggers" may be accompanied by fears that the stressful event will be repeated. Interpersonal relationships often become strained. Greater conflict, such as more frequent arguments with family members and coworkers, is common. On the other hand, you might become withdrawn and isolated and avoid your usual activities. Physical symptoms may accompany the extreme stress. For example, headaches, nausea, and chest pain may result and may require medical attention. Preexisting medical conditions may worsen due to the stress.

(American Psychological Association, 2013).

Resources

APPENDIX

Because resources come and go, new agencies are formed, commercial enterprises merge, and new technologies are developed, the list of resources in this appendix is not exhaustive. However, it does provide an excellent starting point for the identification of mobile applications and sites as well as government, nonprofit, and commercial entities to rely on before, during, and after a disaster.

Websites

Although the Internet has been around since the 1960s, widespread access did not become available until the 1990s. Since then, Internet coverage has become almost ubiquitous, with every major entity, be it public, private, commercial, or personal, establishing a web presence. While increased availability has made it easier to find quality information, it also facilitates the proliferation of sites providing information that is questionable. The websites here are provided to increase the likelihood that libraries get connected to necessary resources at the time they are needed.

Area on Emergency Preparedness and Disaster Relief
http://new.paho.org/disasters/index.php?lang=en
Created by the Pan American Health Organization, this site focuses on assisting public health workers and the general public in Latin America and the Caribbean to be better prepared for common natural disasters such as hurricanes, earthquakes, and volcanoes. Its goal is to lessen the impact of disasters on health.

Services: Disaster planning, disaster recovery

CHEMM (Chemical Hazards Emergency Medical Management)
http://chemm.nlm.nih.gov/
Created by the National Library of Medicine, CHEMM enables first responders and other health-care providers to plan for, respond to, and recover from mass-casualty incidents involving chemical releases. As a web-based resource, CHEMM can be downloaded in advance so that it is always available. Find quick chemical identification, patient care guidelines, initial event activities, and more.

Services: Disaster planning, disaster recovery

Conservation Online (CoOL)

http://cool.conservation-us.org/

CoOL, an online resource operated by the Foundation of the American Institute for Conservation, is a full-text library covering a wide spectrum of topics relevant to the conservation of library, archives, and museum materials. It is an expanding online resource for conservators, collection care specialists, and other conservation professionals. The site includes a link to sample library disaster plans from over 20 libraries.

Services: Conservation, disaster planning

Disaster Mitigation Planning Assistance Website

http://www.matrix.msu.edu/~disaster

This website is a joint project of the Library of Congress Preservation Directorate, the Center for Great Lakes Culture, and the California Preservation Program. Information about where to obtain services and supplies in the event of a disaster is included. Users can search by state, multiple states, or nationally, as well as by type of service, expert, or supply. Search results can be easily downloaded to Excel, which facilitates integration into an institutional disaster plan.

Services: Disaster planning, disaster recovery

Disaster Preparedness for People with Disabilities

http://www.disability911.com/

Created in part by the Independent Living Research Utilization Program, this site was developed to assist, educate, and archive information regarding disaster preparedness for people with disabilities following Hurricanes Katrina and Rita along the Gulf Coast.

Services: Disaster planning

DisasterAssistance.gov

http://www.disasterassistance.gov/

DisasterAssistance.gov offers information in Spanish and English about the availability of federal aid before, during, and after a disaster. Resources help users reduce the number of forms to complete, shorten the time it takes to apply for aid, check the progress of applications online, continue to receive benefits from government programs even after relocating, apply for help from FEMA online, learn about Small Business Administration loans, have Social Security benefits sent to a new address, find federal disaster recovery centers, search a list of housing available for rent, and obtain assistance from the Department of State if disaster strikes while living or traveling abroad.

Services: Disaster planning, disaster recovery

Emergency Preparedness and Response (Centers for Disease Control and Prevention)

http://www.bt.cdc.gov/

The Emergency Preparedness and Response website is the CDC's primary source of information about preparing for and responding to public health emergencies. This site continues to keep the public informed and provides the information needed to protect and save lives.

Services: Disaster planning, disaster recovery

Flu.gov

http://www.flu.gov/

This site includes information about planning for pandemic flu from both the business and personal preparedness perspectives.

Services: Disaster planning

Humane Society Disaster Planning for Pets

http://www.humanesociety.org/news/news/2011/03/disaster_planning_2011.html

This site contains valuable information about preparing animals, including house pets, horses, and livestock, for disasters.

Services: Disaster planning

MedlinePlus

http://www.nlm.nih.gov/medlineplus/

Created by the National Library of Medicine, MedlinePlus offers information on various health concerns, including disaster preparedness and recovery, coping with disasters, and specific disasters such as earthquakes, fires, floods, and hurricanes. Use the search box to identify resources dedicated to a particular subject.

Services: Disaster planning, disaster recovery

Memorial Institute for the Prevention of Terrorism (MIPT) Lawson Library

http://mipt.org/Resources.aspx

MIPT's Lawson Library Police Resources are available to trainees. Information collection, terrorism and crime prevention, and other related topics are included. The library is open access to police officers and the general public as well.

Services: Disaster planning

Minnesota Historical Society Salvage Procedures for Wet Items

http://www.mnhs.org/preserve/conservation/emergency.html

This site offers valuable information on how to salvage numerous types of wet materials, including books with cloth or paper covers, books with leather or vellum covers, magnetic media, microfiche, and paper.

Services: Conservation, disaster recovery

National Incident Management System (NIMS)

http://training.fema.gov/is/nims.asp

NIMS is a structured framework used nationwide for disaster response by both governmental and nongovernmental agencies. This site provides access to the free Incident Command System courses.

Services: Disaster planning, disaster training

National Library of Medicine Specialized Information Services, Special Populations: Emergency and Disaster Preparedness

http://sis.nlm.nih.gov/outreach/specialpopulationsand
disasters.html

Created by the Outreach Activities and Resources section of the U.S. Department of Health and Human Services, this site provides disaster planning information for special populations, including the disabled, seniors, children, and pregnant women. There are also links to information for employers and foreign language materials.

Services: Disaster planning

National Network of Libraries of Medicine (NN/LM) Emergency Preparedness and Response Toolkit

http://nnlm.gov/ep/

Created by the NNLM and the National Library of Medicine, the online toolkit presents a strategy for libraries to develop an emergency response/disaster plan suitable to their environment; establish a backup relationship with a library that can help maintain services during a disaster; and sign an agreement with the backup library that specifies what services will be provided and how the relationship will function.

Services: Disaster planning, disaster training

National Weather Service (NWS)

http://www.weather.gov/

The NWS site offers accurate, up-to-date information on weather throughout the United States, including regional weather, warnings and forecasts, radar, air quality, and satellite maps.

Services: Disaster planning, risk assessment

Public Health Emergency

http://www.phe.gov/preparedness/pages/default.aspx

This site, made available by the U.S. Department of Health and Human Services, Office of the Assistant Secretary for Preparedness and Response, offers breaking news on public health emergencies and preparedness. One program is titled Maximizing State, Local, Tribal and Territorial Awareness through Emerging Technologies.

Services: Disaster planning

Public Health—Seattle and King County Meeting the Needs of Vulnerable Populations/Equity in Emergency Response

http://www.apctoolkits.com/vulnerablepopulation/

Offered by the Seattle and King County Public Health Department and the Advanced Practice Centers of the National Association of County and City Health Officials, this site provides resources and training on emergency planning and response so that no one group is disproportionately affected in an emergency.

Services: Disaster planning, disaster training

Ready.gov

http://www.ready.gov/

Created by FEMA, this website offers practical preparedness information for homes and businesses and includes a special section for kids.

Services: Disaster planning

RSOE EDIS

http://hisz.rsoe.hu/alertmap/

This Hungarian site maps natural and man-made disasters throughout the world. Users can focus on a specific area such as North America or Europe; clickable icons then give real-time information on specific incidents.

Services: Risk assessment

2-1-1

http://www.211.org/

2-1-1 provides free and confidential information and referral for help with evacuation, food, housing, employment, health care, counseling, and more. The site also provides help in locating the nearest agency providing assistance.

Services: Disaster planning

USA.gov

http://www.usa.gov/

The claim of USA.gov is to make government easy. Users can search for specific topics and quickly link to government resources. The search trends feature offers links to popular searches that can include recent disasters. The site also provides various resources for locating family and friends after a major disaster.

Services: Disaster planning, disaster recovery

Weather Channel

http://www.weather.com/

The Weather Channel's website is a good place to go for weather information. The mobile website allows users to pinpoint their location by inputting a ZIP code or using a dropdown list for larger cities worldwide.

Services: Disaster planning, risk assessment

WISER (Wireless Information System for Emergency Responders)

http://wiser.nlm.nih.gov/

Created by the National Library of Medicine, WISER is a system designed to assist first responders with incidents involving hazardous materials. WISER provides a wide range of information on hazardous substances, including substance identification support, physical characteristics, human health information, and containment and suppression advice.

Services: Disaster planning, disaster recovery

Consultants

In the event of a disaster, there are many governmental and noncommercial agencies that can help, but large-scale recovery is difficult without the assistance of commercial vendors. This section lists not-for-profit entities that provide help with risk assessment, disaster planning, mitigation, and recovery.

Governmental or Organizational Consultants

American Institute for Conservation of Historic and Artistic Works (AIC)
http://www.conservation-us.org/
1717 K St. NW, Ste. 200
Washington, DC 20036
(202) 452-9545
AIC plays a crucial role in establishing professional standards, promoting research and publications, providing educational opportunities, and fostering the exchange of knowledge among conservators, allied professionals, and the public. AIC has grown to over 3,500 conservators, educators, scientists, students, archivists, art historians, and other conservation enthusiasts around the world who have the goal to preserve the material evidence of the past.
Services: Conservation, disaster training

American Library Association (ALA)
http://www.ala.org/
50 East Huron St.
Chicago, IL 06011
(800) 545-2433
ALA offers many resources for disaster planning and recovery. The Association for Library Collections and Technical Services (ALCTS) provides a lengthy resource list on its website (http://www.ala.org/ala/mgrps/divs/alcts/confevents/preswk/tools/disaster.cfm). ALA has also offered continuing education seminars on the topic and collected funds to aid libraries that have suffered a disaster.
Services: Disaster training

American Red Cross
http://redcross.org/
8550 Arlington Blvd.
Fairfax, VA 22031
(800) 733-2767
The American Red Cross is the nation's premier emergency response organization, aiding victims of devastating natural disasters. In addition to disaster relief, the American Red Cross offers services in five other areas: community services that help the needy; support and comfort for military members and their families; the collection, processing, and distribution of lifesaving blood and blood products; educational programs that promote health and safety; and international relief and development programs.
Services: Disaster recovery, disaster training

Amigos Library Services
http://www.amigos.org/
14400 Midway Rd.
Dallas, TX 75244
(800) 843-8482
Amigos Library Services is a not-for-profit, membership-based organization dedicated to serving libraries. One service offered is that of disaster planning and recovery. For immediate guidance in the event of an emergency, call the Amigos Imaging and Preservation Service (IPS) to obtain information, referrals to local resources, and on-site assistance. IPS staff members are available to assist with planning activities and recovery from damage caused by various emergency situations, including natural disasters.
Services: Disaster recovery, disaster training

Association for Recorded Sound Collections (ARSC)
http:/www.arsc-audio.org/
PO Box 543
Annapolis, MD 21404
(416) 362-4804
ARSC is a nonprofit organization dedicated to the preservation and study of sound recordings in all genres of music and speech, in all formats, and from all periods. ARSC is unique in bringing together private individuals and institutional professionals with a serious interest in recorded sound. The preservation of sound recordings is one of the primary topics of ARSC publications, conferences, and e-mail discussions.
Services: Media preservation and recovery

Association of Moving Image Archivists (AMIA)
http://www.amianet.org/
1313 North Vine St.
Hollywood, CA 90028
(323) 463-1500
AMIA is a nonprofit professional association established to advance the field of moving image archiving by fostering cooperation among individuals and organizations concerned with the acquisition, description, preservation, exhibition, and use of moving image materials.
Services: Media preservation and recovery

Balboa Art Conservation Center (BACC)
http://www.bacc.org/
1649 El Prado
San Diego, CA 92101
(619) 236-9702
BACC was established as a nonprofit corporation in 1975 to meet the art preservation and restoration needs of cultural, educational, and research institutions in the western region. The up-to-date facilities and highly trained staff at BACC offer institutions access to a broad range of high-quality conservation services at an economical cost.
Services: Preservation services and supplies

Canadian Association of Professional Conservators (CAPC)

http://capc-acrp.ca/index.asp

See website for contact information for board members.

(613) 567-0099

CAPC is a nonprofit association dedicated to the accreditation of professional conservators and the maintenance of high standards in conservation of art and cultural property in Canada. Membership is open to conservators and conservation scientists through defined professional membership requirements.

Services: Disaster training, preservation services and supplies

Canadian Conservation Institute (CCI)

http://www.cci-icc.gc.ca/

1030 Innis Rd.

Ottawa, ON K1A0M5

(613) 998-3721

CCI was created in 1972 to promote the proper care and preservation of Canada's cultural heritage and to advance the practice, science, and technology of conservation. CCI has worked closely with hundreds of organizations to help better preserve collections.

Services: Preservation services and supplies

Chicora Foundation, Inc.

http://www.chicora.org/

PO Box 8664

Columbia, SC 29202

(803) 787-6910

Chicora is a public, nonprofit heritage preservation organization whose work includes archaeological and historical research throughout the southeastern United States; public education; and work in conservation and preservation with museums, libraries, archives, historic organizations, and private citizens.

Services: Preservation services and supplies

Conservation Center for Art and Historic Artifacts (CCAHA)

http://www.ccaha.org/

264 South 23rd St.

Philadelphia, PA 19103

(215) 545-0613

CCAHA specializes in the treatment of paper-based artifacts, including works of art, rare books, photographs, manuscripts, maps, architectural drawings, prints, and historic wallpaper, as well as parchment and papyrus. A state-of-the-art digital imaging studio provides treatment documentation, imaging services, and high-quality facsimiles. CCAHA's staff develops and presents educational programs; conducts preservation assessments and on-site consultations; provides assistance with preservation planning for exhibitions; conducts vulnerability assessments; and develops emergency preparedness plans.

Services: Conservation, disaster planning, disaster training, preservation services and supplies

Council of State Archivists (CoSA)

http://www.statearchivists.org/

308 East Burlington St., Ste. 189

Iowa City, IA 52240

info@statearchivists.org

CoSA is a national organization composed of directors of the principal archival agencies in each state and territorial government. Working collectively, the archivists encourage cooperation on matters of mutual interest, define and communicate archival and records concerns at a national level, and work with the National Historical Publications and Records Commission, National Archives, and other national organizations to ensure that the nation's documentary heritage is preserved and accessible. CoSA developed the disaster planning template discussed in chapter 4.

Services: Conservation, disaster planning

Council of State Historical Records Coordinators (COSHRC)

http://www.coshrc.org/

State contacts are listed on the website.

(518) 473-4254

COSHRC is a national organization composed of State Historical Records Coordinators who define archival and records concerns at a national level and work with other national organizations to ensure that the nation's documentary heritage is preserved and accessible.

Services: Conservation

Disaster Information Management Research Center (DIMRC)

http://disaster.nlm.nih.gov/

8600 Rockville Pike

Bethesda, MD 20894

(301) 496-1131

As part of the National Library of Medicine's Specialized Information Services division, DIMRC is tasked with the collection, organization, and dissemination of health information resources and informatics research related to disasters of natural, accidental, or deliberate origin.

Services: Disaster planning, disaster recovery, disaster training

Emergency Management Institute (EMI)

http://training.fema.gov/emi/

16825 South Seton Ave.

Emmitsburg, MD 21727

(301) 447-1000

EMI is one of several training facilities for the Federal Emergency Management Agency (FEMA) National Incident Management System Incident Command System training and is located on the grounds of the National Emergency Training Center.

Services: Disaster training

Etherington Conservation Services (ECS)
http://www.etheringtoncs.net/
6204 Corporate Park Dr.
Browns Summit, NC 27214
(800) 444-7534
ECS is an internationally recognized conservation laboratory specializing in the preservation and conservation of books, documents, vellum and parchment objects, photographs, and works of art on paper.
Services: Conservation

Federal Emergency Management Agency (FEMA)
http://www.fema.gov/
U.S. Department of Homeland Security
500 C St. SW
Washington, DC 20472
(202) 646-2500
FEMA's mission is to support citizens and first responders to ensure the nation works together to build, sustain, and improve infrastructure and capability to prepare for, protect against, respond to, recover from, and mitigate all hazards. FEMA offers valuable information on planning for and recovering from disasters of all types and financial assistance for qualified businesses and individuals following an event.
Services: Disaster planning, disaster recovery

Gerald R. Ford Conservation Center
http://www.nebraskahistory.org/fordcenter/
1326 South 32nd St.
Omaha, NE 68105
(402) 595-1180
The Ford Center provides preservation services for clients throughout the world, including consultations, assessments of collection needs, surveys of treatment needs, educational and training opportunities, treatment of collection materials, and digital imaging services. Treatment services vary from simple preventive stabilization to complete treatment and cosmetic reintegration.
Services: Conservation

Getty Conservation Institute (GCI)
http://www.getty.edu/conservation/
1200 Getty Center Dr.
Los Angeles, CA 90049
(310) 440-7300
GCI works internationally to advance conservation practice in the visual arts through scientific research, education and training, model field projects, and dissemination of the results of both its own work and the work of others in the field. GCI focuses on the creation and delivery of knowledge that will benefit the professionals and organizations responsible for the conservation of the world's cultural heritage.
Services: Conservation, disaster training

Heritage Preservation
http://222.heritagepreservation.org/
1012 14th St. NW, Ste. 1200
Washington, DC 20005
(202) 233-0800
Heritage Preservation is a national nonprofit organization dedicated to preserving the cultural heritage of the United States. By identifying risks, developing innovative programs, and providing broad public access to expert advice, Heritage Preservation assists museums, libraries, archives, historic preservation and other organizations, and individuals.
Services: Disaster planning, disaster training

Image Permanence Institute (IPI)
http://www.imagepermanenceinstitute.org/
70 Lomb Memorial Dr.
Rochester, NY 14623
(585) 475-5199
IPI is a nonprofit, university-based laboratory devoted to preservation research and is the world's largest independent laboratory with this specific scope. IPI provides information, consulting services, practical tools, and preservation technology to libraries, archives, and museums worldwide. The imaging and consumer preservation industries also use IPI's consulting, testing, and educational services.
Services: Media preservation and recovery

Insurance Information Institute (III)
http://www.iii.org/index.html
110 William St.
New York, NY 10038
(212) 346-5500
The mission of the III is to improve public understanding of insurance, what it does, and how it works. Today, the III is recognized by the media, governments, regulatory organizations, universities, and the public as a primary source of information, analysis, and referral concerning insurance.
Services: Disaster planning, risk assessment

Intermuseum Conservation Association (ICA)
http://www.ica-artconservation.org/
2915 Detroit Ave.
Cleveland, OH 44113
(216) 658-8700
ICA was founded by the directors of six major midwestern museums to provide professional, high-quality, and cost-effective art conservation services. ICA offers climate-controlled storage, custom crate building and display work, surveys and inspections, studio-quality photographic documentation, educational programming, disaster planning and mitigation assistance, grant collaboration, and publications for both professional and general audiences.
Services: Conservation, disaster planning, disaster recovery, disaster training

Library of Congress (LC) Preservation Directorate
http://www.loc.gov/preserv/
101 Independence Ave. SE
Washington, DC 20540
(202) 707-5213
The Preservation Directorate's mission is to ensure long-term, uninterrupted access to the national library collections in original or reformatted form. LC welcomes opportunities for collaborative emergency response networking, education and training, fundraising, outreach, publications, research, and standards development with other preservation-focused organizations on such issues as assessment, risk management, priority setting, exhibition and facility planning, reformatting procedures, stabilization and treatment procedures, and best care practices for special formats of materials.

Services: Conservation, disaster planning, disaster training

LYRASIS (formerly SOLINET)
http://www.lyrasis.org/
1438 West Peachtree St. NW, Ste. 200
Atlanta, GA 30309
(800) 999-8558 or (404) 892-7879
The mission of LYRASIS's Preservation Services is to improve the ability to maintain long-term, cost-effective access to information resources in both traditional and networked collections. LYRASIS provides education and training, information and referral, consultations, and regional coordination. LYRASIS also provides preservation and conservation services such as digital imaging and photo duplication, audio conservation, and emergency response services.

Services: Conservation, disaster planning, disaster training

Midwest Art Conservation Center (MACC)
http://www.preserverart.org/
2400 3rd Ave. South
Minneapolis, MN 55404
(612) 870-3120
MACC is a nonprofit regional center for the preservation and conservation of art and artifacts providing treatment, education, and training for museums, historical societies, libraries, and other cultural institutions. General conservation and preservation services include environmental assessments, collections surveys and storage analysis, training workshops and mentoring, technical information, loans of environmental monitoring equipment, emergency response planning, 24-hour emergency disaster response, and grant writing assistance for preservation and conservation projects.

Services: Conservation

National Archives Preservation Programs
http://www.archives.gov/
8601 Adelphi Rd.
College Park, MD 20740
(866) 272-6272
Preservation Programs at the National Archives consist of two units committed to the physical well-being of federal records in the custody of the National Archives and Records Administration. The Document Conservation Laboratory is responsible for conservation activities that contribute to the prolonged usable life of records in their original format. The Special Media Preservation Laboratory is responsible for reformatting and duplicating records created in textual and nontextual formats.

Services: Conservation, media preservation and recovery

National Center for Animal Health Emergency Management (NCAHEM)
http://www.aphis.usda.gov/animal_health/emergency_management/
U.S. Department of Agriculture
4700 River Rd., Unit 41
Riverdale, MD 20737
(301) 734-8073
(800) 940-6524 (emergency only)
As leaders in animal health emergency management, NCAHEM develops strategies and policies for effective incident management and helps coordinate incident responses. As a liaison to outside emergency management groups, it ensures that veterinary services emergency management policies, strategies, and responses reflect national and international standards.

Services: Disaster planning

National Emergency Management Association (NEMA)
http://www.nemaweb.org/
PO Box 11910
Lexington, KY 40578
(859) 244-8000
NEMA is a nonpartisan, nonprofit 501(c)(3) organization dedicated to enhancing public safety by improving the nation's ability to prepare for, respond to, and recover from all emergencies, disasters, and threats to national security. NEMA provides leadership and expertise in comprehensive emergency management; serves as a vital emergency management information and assistance resource; and advances continuous improvement in emergency management through strategic partnerships, innovative programs, and collaborative policy positions.

Services: Disaster planning, disaster recovery

National Fire Protection Association (NFPA)
http://www.nfpa.org/
1 Batterymarch Park
Quincy, MA 02169
(617) 770-3000
The mission of the international nonprofit NFPA is to reduce the worldwide burden of fire and other hazards on the quality of life by providing standards, research, training, and education. The world's leading advocate of fire prevention and an authoritative source on public safety, NFPA develops, publishes, and disseminates more than 300 consensus codes and standards intended to minimize the possibility and effects of fire and other risks.
Services: Disaster planning

National Flood Insurance Program (NFIP)
http://www.fema.gov/business/nfip/
500 C St. SW
Washington, DC 20472
(202) 646-2500
As part of FEMA, the three components of the NFIP are flood insurance, floodplain management, and flood hazard mapping. This agency assists with disaster planning, recovery and rebuilding, and mapping information on various types of disasters.
Services: Disaster planning, disaster recovery

National Hurricane Center (NHC)
http://www.nhc.noaa.gov/
11691 SW 17th St.
Miami, FL 33165
(305) 229-4522
The NHC is the division of the National Weather Service responsible for predicting and tracking weather systems in the tropics. During hurricane season the NHC monitors the Atlantic and Pacific Oceans, as well as the Gulf of Mexico, and issues appropriate watches and warnings. The website provides guidance on planning for a hurricane and evacuation tips.
Services: Disaster planning

National Voluntary Organization Active in a Disaster (National VOAD)
http://nvoad.org/
1501 Lee Hwy., Ste. 170
Arlington, VA 22209
(703) 778-5088
National VOAD is a forum for organizations to share knowledge and resources throughout the disaster cycle and help disaster survivors and their communities. This forum seeks to facilitate a more organized response and minimize unnecessary duplication.
Services: Disaster planning, disaster recovery

Northeast Document Conservation Center (NEDCC)
http://www.nedcc.org/
100 Brickstone Sq.
Andover, MA 01801
(978) 470-1010
NEDCC is one of the largest nonprofit, regional conservation centers in the United States, specializing in the preservation and conservation of paper-based materials for collections-holding institutions. NEDCC conducts general preservation assessments; presents workshops, conferences, and training programs in the United States and abroad; answers reference inquiries; and provides free 24-hour disaster assistance.
Services: Conservation, disaster recovery, disaster training

Pan American Health Organization (PAHO) Area on Emergency Preparedness and Disaster Relief
http://new.paho.org/disasters/index.php?lang=en
525 23rd St. NW
Washington, DC 20037
(202) 974-3000
PAHO, a division of the World Health Organization, works with member countries to improve disaster preparedness in the health sector, protect health services from the risk of disasters, support countries in responding to health needs during emergencies, and strengthen partnerships with national and international participants.
Services: Disaster planning, disaster recovery

Regional Alliance for Preservation (RAP)
http://rap-arcc.org/
Member contacts are available on the website.
RAP is a national network of nonprofit organizations with expertise in conservation and preservation. Through coordinated outreach activities, educational programs, and publications, RAP organizations foster awareness about preserving cultural heritage. RAP members present training programs, provide conservation and preservation services, create publications to assist institutions in caring for collections, and provide free technical advice to collecting institutions around the United States.
Services: Conservation, disaster planning, disaster training

West Lake Conservators
http://westlakeconservators.com/
Skaneateles, NY 13152
(315) 685-8534
West Lake Conservators is a nationally recognized firm specializing in the preservation and restoration of historic and artistic works, including paintings, frames, murals, textiles, paper, and photographs.
Services: Conservation

Western States and Territories Preservation Assistance Service (WESTPAS)
http://westpas.org/info@westpas.org
WESTPAS is a regional library and archives preservation service with the goal of offering preservation education and training workshops in 14 participating states and territories: Alaska, American Samoa, California, Colorado, Guam, Hawaii, Idaho, Montana, Nevada, Northern Mariana Islands, Oregon, Utah, Washington, and Wyoming. In addition to training, WESTPAS maintains a 24/7 disaster assistance number to provide advice and help in the event of a collection disaster.

Services: Disaster planning, disaster recovery, disaster training

World Association for Disaster and Emergency Management (WADEM)
http://www.wadem.org/
PO Box 55158
Madison, WI 53705
(608) 819-6604
WADEM is a nonoperational, nongovernmental organization with a primary focus on education and research. WADEM's membership is composed of physicians, nurses, professors, paramedics, EMTs, psychologists, social workers, students, dentists, sociologists, emergency planners and managers, and public health officials representing 55 countries. A glossary of disaster-related terms can be found at http://www.wadem .org/guidelines/glossary.pdf.

Services: Disaster planning, disaster training

Commercial Consultants

ADR Data Recovery
http://www.adrdatarecovery.com/
23 North Second St.
Hamilton, MT 59840
(800) 450-9282
ADR offers data recovery for laptops, desktops, and external hard drives, as well as RAIS data recovery and the restoration of vital business data from offline and failed servers.

Services: Data storage and recovery

Aeroscopic Environmental
http://www.aeroscopic.com/
1833 Dana St.
Glendale, CA 91201
(818) 543-3930
Aeroscopic specializes in health, safety, and environmental services; sick building syndrome; odor and pollution control; structure and content cleaning; HVAC cleaning; and computer and document reclamation.

Services: Data storage and recovery, disaster recovery, environmental control

Aggreko
http://www.aggreko.com/
120 Bothwell St.
Glasgow G2 7JS
(800) 603-6021
A global company with offices worldwide, Aggreko provides temporary power generation, temperature control, and compressed air systems. With over 100 locations in 29 countries (over 50 in North America alone), Aggreko offers 24/7/365 service in climate control.

Services: Disaster recovery, environmental control, temperature and humidity control

Agility Recovery Solutions
http://www2.agilityrecovery.com/
2101 Rexford Rd., Ste. 350E
Charlotte, NC 28211
(866) 364-9696
In the event of a disaster, Agility Recovery Solutions offers four key elements of business continuity: power, technology, space, and connectivity. Formerly known as GE Disaster Recovery Services, Agility has 21 years of disaster recovery experience.

Services: Data storage and retrieval, disaster recovery, power generation

Air Quality Sciences, Inc. (AQS)
http://www.aqs.com/
2211 Newmarket Pkwy.
Atlanta, GA 30067
(770) 933-0638
AQS deals with indoor air quality testing, building studies, and building certification plan development. Services include testing for occupant health complaints, water-damaged materials, mold and chemical contamination, odor concerns, and acceptance of newly constructed, renovated, or remediated buildings. They also assist in green building design.

Services: Environmental control, mold remediation, temperature and humidity control

American Freeze-Dry Operations, Inc.
http://www.americanfreezedry.com/
1722 Hurffville Rd., Bldg. 2A
Five Points Business Center
Sewell, NJ 08080
(856) 939-8160
American Freeze-Dry Operations, Inc. was established in 1976 with an original focus on processing water- and mold-infected archival material and library volumes. The company services have expanded to the restoration of government documents, attorney files, and medical records.

Services: Freeze-drying

American Interfile and Library Services
http://www.americaninterfile.com/
55 Sweeneydale Ave.
Bayshore, NY 11706
(800) 426-9901
American Interfile is a company that specializes in relocating library materials, especially in the construction of a new facility or in a renovation; however, the company's services can also be valuable after a disaster if materials have to be relocated temporarily or permanently.
Services: Disaster recovery

Americold
http://www.americoldrealty.com/
10 Glenlake Pkwy., South Tower, Ste. 800
Atlanta, GA 30328
(678) 441-1400
Americold offers comprehensive warehousing, transportation, and logistic solutions with over 182 temperature-controlled warehouses in the United States, Australia, New Zealand, China, Argentina, and Canada. The company's combined storage capacity is approximately 1.1 billion cubic square feet.
Services: Freeze-drying

ANSUL
http://www.ansul.com/
1 Stanton St.
Marinette, WI 54143
(800) 862-6785
ANSUL offers fire protection solutions including fire extinguishers, pre-engineered corporate solutions, and fire detection and suppression systems with dry, chemical, foam, and gaseous extinguishing agents.
Services: Fire suppression

Archival Products
http://www.archival.com/
PO Box 1413
Des Moines, IA 50306
(800) 526-5640
Archival Products provides preservation solutions for libraries, colleges and universities, museums, historical societies, medical schools, government offices, and consumers.
Services: Preservation services and supplies

Archivart
http://www.archivart.com/
40 Eisenhower Dr.
Paramus, NJ 07652
(800) 804-8428
Archivart offers archival products for conservation treatments, exhibitions, and artifact storage.
Services: Preservation services and supplies

Art Preservation Services (APS)
http://apsnyc.com/
44–45 Vernon Blvd.
Long Island City, NY 11101
(347) 612-4584
APS specializes in the environmental preservation of collections in archives, museums, and historic buildings. APS also supports research and development in the areas of relative humidity, light, air pollution, monitoring, data logging, and environmental condition alarms.
Services: Preservation services and supplies

Atlantic Paste and Glue Company (AP&G)
http://www.catchmasterpro.com/
170 53rd St.
Brooklyn, NY 11232
(800) 458-7454
AP&G focuses on pest management applications, including the control of rodents and insects.
Services: Pest control

Bacharach, Inc.
http://www.bacharach-inc.com/
621 Hunt Valley Cir.
New Kensington, PA 15068
(800) 736-4666
Bacharach, Inc. designs, manufactures, and tests instruments that detect, measure, and record air quality, temperature, and humidity with regard to safety parameters. The company also offers refrigerant recovery equipment.
Services: Environmental control, freeze-drying

Barracuda Networks
http://www.barracudanetworks.com/
3175 Winchester Blvd.
Campbell, CA 95008
(888) 268-4772
Barracuda offers full local data backups with server options for off-site data replication. To prevent catastrophic data loss, replication backups to the cloud, to privately owned locations, or to a combination of both are also options.
Services: Data storage and retrieval

BELFOR USA
http://belforusa.com/
Refer to the website for regional and international offices.
(800) 856-3333
In business for over 35 years, BELFOR is a leader in property restoration and repair with an extensive network of resources for homes or businesses. No matter how extensive the damage, BELFOR can dispatch response teams and equipment from many U.S. locations.
Services: Dehumidification, disaster recovery, environmental control, power generation

Blackmon Mooring Steamatic (BMS)
http://www.blackmooring.com/
Refer to the website for regional offices.
(800) 624-6179
Originally started in 1948 as a furniture and dye shop, BMS now offers fire damage restoration, water damage restoration, and mold remediation to business and residential customers.
Services: Dehumidification, disaster recovery, environmental control, power generation

Blast, Inc.
http://www.kccold.com/
16500 East Truman Rd.
Independence, MO 64050
(800) 892-7019
Blast, Inc. provides cold storage and refrigerated trucks to assist with wet collections following a flood or fire.
Services: Freeze-drying

CBL Data Recovery Technologies, Inc.
http://www.cbldatarecovery.com/
2250 Satellite Blvd., Ste. 240
Duluth, GA 30097
(800) 551-3917
CBL Data Recovery Technologies, Inc. provides data recovery services for failed hard disk drives in laptops, desktops, servers, RAID arrays, and tape cartridges.
Services: Data storage and retrieval

Chubb Services Corporation
http://www.chubb.com/
15 Mountain View Rd.
Warren, NJ 07059
(908) 903-2000
Chubb Services Corporation provides claims, loss control, disaster recovery planning services, and managed care solutions. Risk management services include claim management for self-insured companies, deductible insurance programs, self-insured groups, and captive groups.
Services: Disaster planning, risk assessment

Conney Safety
http://www.conney.com/
3202 Latham Dr.
Madison, WI 53744
(888) 356-9100
Conney Safety offers a full line of safety equipment, including first aid supplies, eye protection, protective clothing, gas detection and instrumentation, and janitorial supplies.
Services: Disaster supplies

Crowley Company
http://www.thecrowleycompany.com/
5111 Pegasus Ct., Ste. M
Frederick, MD 21704
(240) 215-0224

The Crowley Company blends manufacturer, distributor, and service bureaus. The company offers a range of digital and analog solutions for imaging technology and film processing, including hardware, imaging services, systems consulting, supplies, and technical support.
Services: Disaster supplies, media preservation and recovery

Cutting Corporation
http://wwwcuttingarchives.com/
4940 Hampden Ln., Ste. 300
Bethesda, MD 20814
(301) 654-2887
The Cutting Corporation provides a full-service archival lab capable of both audio preservation (accurate re-recording) and audio restoration (removing distortion, recovering signal loss, or recovering signal decay).
Services: Media preservation and recovery

Data Retrieval Phoenix
http://www.dataretrieval.com/
40 North Central Ave., Ste. 1400
Phoenix, AZ 85004
(800) 399-7150
Data Retrieval restores data from any type of storage media, including hard drives, external and flash drives, magnetic tapes, solid state disks, CD and DVD ROM drives, and RAID arrays of any level.
Services: Media preservation and recovery

Document Reprocessors
http://www.documentreprocessors.com/
West Coast Facility
1384 Rollins Rd.
Burlingame, CA 94010
(650) 401-7711
East Coast Facility
40 Railroad Ave.
Rushville, NY 14544
(585) 554-4500
Document Reprocessors specializes in the restoration of books, documents, and magnetic/micrographic media. Mobile vacuum freeze-drying equipment is available and can be transported to a disaster site.
Services: Disaster recovery, freeze-drying, media preservation and recovery

Dorlen Products, Inc.
http://www.wateralert.com/
6615 West Layton Ave.
Milwaukee, WI 53220
(414) 282-4840
Dorlen Products, Inc. provides simple and reliable water-leak detection equipment and systems.
Services: Environmental control

DuPont Safety and Protection
http://www2.dupont.com/Safety_and_Protection/en_US/
Chestnut Run Plaza
Wilmington, DE 19880
(800) 441-7515
DuPont Safety and Protection offers science-based solutions focused on the protection of people, property, operations, and the environment.
Services: Environmental control

Dust Free
http://www.dustfree.com/
1112 Industrial Dr.
Royse City, TX 75189
(800) 441-1107
Dust Free manufactures air purification equipment for both residential and business applications. The company also provides indoor air quality training and has an active research and development program designed to meet the indoor air quality needs of the future.
Services: Environmental control

Eastman Kodak Disaster Recovery Program
http://www.kodak.com/
1901 West 22nd St.
Oak Brook, IL 60652
(800) 352-8378
The Kodak Disaster Recovery Program rescues and restores damaged film. Consultations are available 24/7; lab personnel will respond quickly to assess the situation following a disaster.
Services: Media preservation and recovery

EPIC Response
http://www.epicrsponse.com/
3045 Chastain Meadows Pkwy., Ste. 400
Marietta, GA 30066
(877) 277-4647
EPIC Response works with clients before, during, and after a disaster to develop a complete preincident plan that can dramatically decrease response time, recovery time, and cost. EPIC is always on standby to respond regardless of the scope of the emergency.
Services: Disaster planning, disaster recovery

Film Technology Company, Inc.
http://ww.filmtech.com/
726 North Cole Ave.
Los Angeles, CA
(323) 464-3456
Film Technology Company, Inc. has restored thousands of motion pictures. Services include restoring motion picture archives of libraries, museums, historical societies, universities, government agencies, and foundations.
Services: Media preservation and recovery

First Choice Drying Equipment Sales and Service
http://www.firstchoicedryingequipment.com/
906 L St.
Penrose, CO 81240
(719) 372-0990
First Choice Drying Equipment Sales and Service supplies dehumidifiers, desiccant dehumidifier products, accessories, and air movement systems designed for technically complex applications in both industrial and commercial markets.
Services: Environmental control

Halotron, Inc.
http://www.halotron.com/
3883 Howard Hughes Pkwy., Ste. 700
Las Vegas, NV 89169
(702) 735-2200
Halotron, Inc. manufactures halocarbon-based fire extinguishing agents with a wide variety of commercial and industrial applications. The company's products are clean agents that are discharged as a rapidly evaporating liquid or gas, minimizing potential agent-related damage to valuable assets.
Services: Fire suppression

Industrial Cold Storage (ICS)
http://icslogistics.com/
2625 West Fifth St.
Jacksonville, FL 32203
(904) 786-8038
ICS's customs-bonded warehouse facility in Jacksonville provides 8,200,000 cubic feet of racked refrigerated storage and blast freezing services.
Services: Freeze-drying

Insects Limited, Inc.
http://www.insectslimited.com/
16950 Westfield Park Rd.
Westfield, IN 46074
(317) 896-9300
Insects Limited, Inc. researches, tests, develops, manufactures, and distributes pheromones and trapping systems for stored product insects. Staff members can also assist with consultations, serve as expert witnesses, and present training.
Services: Pest control

Kidde-Fenwall
http://www.kidde-fenwal.com/
400 Main St.
Ashland, MA 01721
(508) 881-2000
Kidde-Fenwell is a leading fire protection manufacturer that designs and manufactures temperature controls and heat detection systems for commercial, industrial, and institutional entities.
Services: Fire suppression

MBK Consulting
http://www.mbkcons.com/
60 North Harding Rd.
Columbus, OH 43209
(614) 239-8977
MBK Consulting offers a variety of services, including training, consulting, and research for libraries, archives, historical societies, and other organizations. Workshop topics include preservation of library materials, book repair, repair of archival and manuscript collections, disaster response, and prevention planning.
Services: Disaster planning, disaster training

Midwest Freeze Dry, Ltd.
http://www.midwestfreezedry.com/
7326 North Central Park
Skokie, IL 60076
(847) 679-4756
Midwest Freeze Dry deals with the restoration and conservation of damaged documents. Services include freeze-drying, mold remediation, pest infestation fumigation, and odor removal.
Services: Freeze-drying

New Pig
http://www.newpig.com/
One Pork Ave.
Tipton, PA 16684
(800) 468-4647
New Pig offers a wide array of safety products, including leak diverters and ceiling repair, air and liquid filtration, trash and recycling containers, gloves and arm protection, hearing and head protection, safety glasses, and first aid kits.
Services: Safety products

Orkin
http://www.orkin.com/
See the website for locations.
(866) 949-6097
Orkin is a nationwide pest control company that treats for ants, mice, mosquitoes, fleas, spiders, bedbugs, flies, termites, cockroaches, rats, crickets, and ticks.
Services: Pest control

Page, Julie
julieallenpage@gmail.com
(760) 224-0419
As an independent library disaster consultant, Ms. Page is the founder of SILDRN (San Diego/Imperial County Libraries Disaster Response Network), has co-coordinated the California preservation program since 1998, and is cofounder of WESTPAS. She has extensive experience with disaster preparedness and response training. She is available for response to library emergencies of any type.
Services: Disaster planning, disaster recovery, disaster training

Pest Control Services, Inc.
http://www.termitesonly.com/
469 Mimosa Cir.
Kennett Square, PA 19348
(610) 444-2277
Pest Control Services, Inc. is an entomological consulting practice in the structural pest control industry. A major area of expertise is the inspection and analysis of actual and potential pest problems for libraries, museums, archives, historic properties, and their collections. Workshops and presentations for professional audiences are also available.
Services: Pest control

Polygon
http://www.munters.com/
79 Monroe St.
Amesbury, MA 01913
(800) 843-5360
Formerly known as Munters, Polygon provides products and services for water and fire damage restoration, dehumidification, humidification, and air cooling.
Services: Dehumidification, disaster recovery, environmental control

ProTEXT
http://www.protext.com/
PO Box 864
Greenfield, MA 01302
(301) 320-7231
The mission of ProTEXT is to minimize the damage caused by natural or man-made disasters by providing collection caretakers with appropriate supplies and information.
Services: Disaster planning, disaster supplies

Rackspace
http://www.rackspace.com/
5000 Walzem Rd.
San Antonio, TX 78218
(800) 961-2888
Rackspace offers digital hosting solutions, including managed, cloud, and hybrid hosting services for businesses of all sizes and kinds around the world.
Services: Data storage and recovery

Reliable Automatic Sprinkler Company, Inc.
http://www.reliablesprinkler.com/
103 Fairview Park Dr.
Elmsford, NY 10523
(800) 431-1588
Reliable Automatic Sprinkler Company, Inc. manufactures automatic fire sprinklers, valve and accessory products, and sprinkler system components.
Services: Fire suppression

Mobile Technologies

Apps

American Medical Aid

https://itunes.apple.com/us/app/american-medical-aid/
id303689017?mt=8/
iPhone, iPod touch, iPad
American Medical Aid provides detailed, illustrated instructions for a variety of emergencies. Users can also create a customized medical profile.

Services: Emergencies, personal data

American Red Cross: Shelter View

https://itunes.apple.com/us/app/american-red-cross-shelter/
id419258261?mt=8/
iPhone, iPod touch, iPad
Users in need of shelter following a disaster can locate where facilities have been opened. Maps of shelter locations are provided.

Services: Directory

Complete Home First Aid

http://www.redivideos.com/hfa.php/
iPhone, iPad, Android, BlackBerry
This app includes directions, images, and videos for a number of emergency situations, such as diabetic emergencies, poisons, stroke, and choking. Information on CPR, splints and slings, and use of the EpiPen is also provided.

Services: Emergencies

Disaster Prep

http://itunes.apple.com/us/app/disaster-prep/
id431738659?mt=8/
iPhone, iPod touch, iPad
This app, developed through funding from the San Luis Obispo County Public Health Department's Emergency Preparedness Office, provides guidance about preparing a disaster kit as well as information about basic CPR, first aid, and general considerations for preparedness, response, and recovery. Also included are the *U.S. Military Survival Manual* and the ability to record and store personal health data as well as insurance and vehicle information.

Services: Disaster planning, disaster recovery, emergencies, personal data, reference material

Earthquake

http://www.mobeezio.com/apps/earthquake/
iPhone, iPod touch, iPad
Users can monitor earthquakes all over the world in real time with this app. Features include live data from the U.S. Geological Survey (USGS), integration with Google Maps, the ability to e-mail screenshots of maps and data about events, and the option to report earthquakes directly to the USGS website.

Services: Alerts/communication, GPS/navigation services, reference material

Earthquake Survival Kit

http://www.earthquake-survival-kit.net/
iPhone, iPod touch, iPad
This app includes an alarm that sounds when an earthquake is detected and SOS signals that could be seen and/or heard by rescue crews. Safety tips in the event of an earthquake, general information about earthquakes, and basic first aid techniques are also provided.

Services: Alerts/communication, reference material

Emergency Distress Beacon

http://cinndev.com/emergency.php/
iPhone, iPad
Upon activation, this app will send out a distress beacon and the user's current location to those who need to know.

Services: Alerts/communication, emergencies, personal data

Emergency Radio

http://www.edgerift.com/emergencyradio/
iPhone, iPod touch
Listen to live emergency frequencies including police, fire, medical, weather, and traffic. Users can utilize the "Nearby" feature to locate frequencies in the area or browse a list of all available frequencies.

Services: Alerts/communication

EZ Radar

http://www.iphoneezproducts.com/iphoneezproducts/
EZ_Radar.html/
iPhone
Available for particular states or regions (EZ Radar-OK/AR, EZ Radar-TX, etc.), this app provides animated radar direct from the National Weather Service via one-touch access.

Services: Weather information

Facebook

http://www.facebook.com/mobile/
iPhone, Android, BlackBerry, Palm, Windows Phone
Facebook users have a number of mobile options in addition to apps, all of which are outlined on this mobile page.

Services: Alerts/communication

1st Response: Be Prepared

https://itunes.apple.com/us/app/1st-response-be-prepared/
id300102561?mt=8/
iPhone, iPad, iPod
This app is designed to assist the user in emergency situations. Features include concise, easy to follow instructions for many disasters, links to external agencies and call centers, a customizable personal profile, and lights, distress signal, and emergency 911 call functions.

Services: Disaster recovery, emergencies, personal data

5-0 Radio Pro Police Scanner

http://smartestapple.com/

iPhone, iPod touch, iPad

Users can listen to police scanners worldwide and create a list of favorites for easy access.

Services: *Alerts/communication*

FloodWatch

http://www.floodwatchapp.com/

iPhone, iPod touch, iPad

Users can monitor rivers and streams in their area, viewing both recent and historic information about river heights, flood stage, and precipitation cumulated from U.S. Geological Survey and National Weather Service data.

Services: *Weather information*

Health Hotlines

http://healthhotlines.nlm.nih.gov/

iPhone, iPod touch, iPad

Created and maintained by the National Library of Medicine, this app allows users to search or browse for health-oriented organizations that have toll-free numbers. Information on services in Spanish is also available.

Services: *Directory*

Here I Am

http://www.youtube.com/watch?v=Og-XHfvc33I/

iPhone, Android

Users can send their current location to anyone in their address book.

Services: *Alerts/communication, GPS/navigation*

Hurricane Pro

http://kittycode.com/products/hurricane/

iPhone, iPad

Track active storms through interactive maps, animated satellites and radar images, and information from the National Hurricane Center. This app also provides historical information on all hurricanes back to 1851 in the Atlantic and to 1949 in the Pacific.

Services: *Weather information*

ICEcare

http://icecare.net/home.aspx/

iPhone, iPod touch, iPad, Android, BlackBerry, Palm, Windows Mobile

Information about medical conditions, allergies, current medications, emergency contacts, and other user-specific health information can be stored utilizing this app. Also included are preparedness and emergency planning information.

Services: *Disaster planning, personal data*

iFeltThat

http://dannyg.com/iapps/iFeltThat.html

iPhone, iPod touch, iPad

Users can obtain an overview of earthquake activity by browsing 24 regions worldwide. The most recent events are at the top of the list, and regions in the United States include very specific location information. Roadmaps and satellite map views are available. Direct access to U.S. Geological Survey Shake Maps and other data as well as tsunami information from the National Oceanic and Atmospheric Administration is also provided.

Services: *Alerts/communication, reference material*

iFirstAid

http://ifirstaid.com/

iPhone, iPod touch, iPad

Features of this app include information on resuscitation/CPR, bleeding, choking, stroke, poisons, and a number of other first aid topics. Links to quick-dial emergency numbers and region-specific information are also provided.

Services: *Alerts/communication, emergencies, reference material*

iGetThru

http://igetthru.appspot.com/

iPhone, iPod touch, iPad

This app is designed to help users build and maintain an emergency kit. Items are divided into a number of categories such as Food and Water, Personal Items, Family Documents, and Children's Items. Each category contains a list of specific items that should be included in the kit. Users are alerted to missing items, and calendar reminders are added for items with expiration dates, such as food, bottled water, and medicines. Lists can be customized based on a user's specific needs. Also included are alerting and location-based services for the user and designated individuals, as well as general and disaster-specific emergency information.

Services: *Alerts/communication, disaster planning, emergencies*

iSOS Alert

http://www.isosalert.com/

iPhone, Android

Users can send location information to family, police, medical personnel, and others in the event of an emergency.

Services: *GPS/navigation services*

iSurvive

http://www.isurviverescueapp.com/

iPhone

This app provides GPS tracking, SMS alerts, and additional features for both attacks and accidental emergencies.

Services: *Emergencies, GPS/navigation services*

Life360

https://www.life360.com/free

iPhone, Android

This app allows users to track, in real time, the location of family members as well as receive and send alerts if a family member needs assistance.

Services: GPS/navigation services

911 Police Radio

http://www.freetheapps.com/our-apps/911-police-radio-free/

iPhone, iPad

This app connects users to a substantial, live network of emergency radio stations, including channels provided by law enforcement, firefighters, and other first responders.

Services: Alerts/communication

Outbreaks Near Me

http://healthmap.org/outbreaksnearme/

iPhone, Android

Features allow users to track disease outbreaks around the world and receive alerts when an outbreak occurs close to home.

Services: Alerts/communication

Pillbox

http://pillboxapp.com/

iPhone, iPod touch, iPad

Users can manage a list of personal medications as well as medication profiles for family members. Each medication entered is linked to a database providing additional information.

Services: Personal data, reference material

Pocket First Aid and CPR

http://jive.me/apps/firstaid/

iPhone, iPod touch, iPad, Android

Through text, illustrations, and videos this app provides information from the American Heart Association on CPR and a variety of first aid emergencies, including choking, bites, seizures, and cuts/wounds. Users can also save personal medical and insurance information.

Services: Emergencies, personal data

PTSD Coach

http://www.ptsd.va.gov/Public/pages/PTSDCoach.asp/

iPhone, iPod touch, iPad, Android

Created by the Veterans Administration's National Center for PTSD and the Department of Defense's National Center for Telehealth and Technology, this app provides information on PTSD, screening, and treatment options. Users can track their symptoms and review skills to help them manage their diagnosis. Direct links to support and resources are also provided.

Services: Alerts/communication, reference material, risk assessment

Radiation Emergency Medical Management (REMM)

http://www.remm.nlm.gov/downloadmremm.htm/

iPhone, iPod touch, Android, BlackBerry, Palm, Windows Mobile

This app is designed for health-care providers and includes information about the diagnosis and treatment of radiation injuries resulting from radiological and nuclear disasters. The mobile version contains selected files from the full online version, which is produced by the Department of Health and Human Services, Office of Planning and Emergency Response, in cooperation with the National Library of Medicine.

Services: Reference material

Relief Central

http://relief.unboundmedicine.com/relief/ub

iPhone, iPod touch, iPad, Android, BlackBerry, Palm, Windows Mobile

This is a resource portal designed for anyone who is called to respond to disasters around the world. The app provides access to *The World Factbook* from the U.S. Central Intelligence Agency, the U.S. Agency for International Development's *Field Operations Guide for Disaster Assessment and Response*, and RSS feeds from a variety of relief organizations, including the Red Cross and FEMA. Access to journal literature from the MEDLINE database is also incorporated into the portal.

Services: Reference material

ReUnite

http://archive.nlm.nih.gov/proj/lpf.php/

iPhone, iPod touch, iPad

While this app is intended for use by workers assisting with reuniting families following a disaster, it is also available to anyone wishing to report people who are missing or found.

Services: Personal data

Send.Morse

http://iphone.reizverstaerker.at/

iPhone, iPod touch, iPad

This app enables the real-time transmission of text into Morse code and the capability to decode received light signals back into text.

Services: Alerts/communication

smart-ICE (In Case of Emergency)

http://www.ems-options.com/

iPhone, iPod touch, iPad

Features include the ability to record a message with essential medical information if the user is incapable of interacting with emergency personnel, "Alert EMS" and "My Location" functionality, and the option to store a detailed, personal health history profile. The smart-ICE4family app gives users the option to create up to eight profiles.

Services: Alert/communication, personal data

SOS! Emergency Preparedness

http://7grapes.com/default.aspx/
iPhone, iPod touch, iPad
Users can store personal health, insurance, and emergency information, map hospitals, and access information about first aid and disaster preparedness.

Services: Disaster planning, personal data

Twitter

http://twitter.com/#!/download/
iPhone, iPad, Android, BlackBerry, Windows Phone 7
Users can access Twitter from a variety of mobile devices by downloading the app or by visiting the mobile-optimized site at http://mobile.twitter.com/.

Services: Alerts/communication

USHospFinder

https://itunes.apple.com/us/app/ushospfinder/id412630399/
iPhone, iPod touch, iPad
This app identifies the closest U.S. hospital utilizing the user's location. Results are displayed based on proximity and include an interactive map with driving directions and one-touch access to the hospital's phone number and website.

Services: Directory, GPS/navigation services

Weather Alert USA

http://www.softpeas.com/
iPhone, iPod touch, iPad
This app enables users to access the National Oceanic and Atmospheric Administration's weather information providing alerts, maps, and summaries of major events.

Services: Weather information

WISER (Wireless Information System for Emergency Responders)

http://wiser.nlm.nih.gov/
iPhone, iPod touch, iPad, Android, BlackBerry
WISER is designed to provide essential information to first responders who are called in to handle incidents involving hazardous materials. Users can search by a specific substance or browse categories; information provided includes substance identification assistance, physical properties, containment/suppression support, and information about the human health effects.

Services: Reference material

Mobile-Optimized Websites

Google Mobile

http://www.google.com/mobile/
Google has a number of mobile applications and services that are summarized on this page. Availability will vary by the type of device, but Google makes it easy to figure out the possibilities.

Services: Alerts/communication, reference material

MedlinePlus

http://m.medlineplus.gov/
This site provides access to a version of the National Library of Medicine's consumer health information website optimized for mobile devices. Users will find information on numerous health topics, prescription and nonprescription drugs, a medical dictionary, and current health news.

Services: Reference material

Mobile CDC

http://m.cdc.gov/
The mobile site for the Centers for Disease Control and Prevention features brief updates on health observances, grants, training, and upcoming events. Also provided is quick access to a variety of topics relevant to health and safety, including emergency preparedness and response information.

Services: Reference material

National Weather Service

http://mobile.weather.gov/
Users on the go can obtain local weather facts by entering their city or ZIP code as well as gain access to weather advisories, reports from regional radars, and satellite images.

Services: Weather information

PubMed Mobile

http://www.ncbi.nlm.nih.gov/m/pubmed/
Users can search MEDLINE/PubMed through this portal optimized for mobile devices.

Services: Reference material

YouTube for Mobile

http://www.google.com/mobile/youtube/
Users can search or browse for videos, upload their own content, provide comments, and access their YouTube accounts from a variety of mobile devices.

Services: Alerts/communication, reference material

About the Authors

Deborah Halsted has over 30 years of professional library experience, primarily in academic medical libraries. It was after severe flooding in the Texas Medical Center Library in Houston caused by Tropical Storm Allison in 2001 that she became involved in disaster planning and recovery. In 2005 she coauthored *Disaster Planning: A How-To-Do-It Manual for Librarians* based on her personal experiences. She has remained active in disaster planning, especially in extensive training in the National Incident Management System Incident Command System, which is vital to any incident, large or small. She received her master's degree in library science from Florida State University.

Shari Clifton has been a health sciences librarian for more than 20 years and is currently Professor/Head of Reference and Instructional Services at the University of Oklahoma Health Sciences Center's Robert M. Bird Library in Oklahoma City, Oklahoma. An active participant in professional organizations at the state, regional, and national levels, Clifton has held a variety of elected/appointed positions and has presented numerous papers, posters, and programs at professional meetings. She is a distinguished member of the Medical Library Association's Academy of Health Information Professionals. For many years, Clifton has served as the coordinator of outreach activities for the Bird Library, and she has been actively involved in preparedness activities in Oklahoma and her region. In addition, she directs mediated search services and support for individuals working on systematic reviews and other comprehensive projects. Clifton earned her master's degree in library and information science from the University of Oklahoma in Norman, Oklahoma.

Daniel Wilson is the associate director for Collections and Library Services at the University of Virginia Claude Moore Health Sciences Library. Since the summer of 2007, he has served as the coordinator for the National Network of Libraries of Medicine (NN/LM) National Emergency Preparedness and Response Initiative. In that role, Dan coordinates the emergency preparedness and response activates of the network and regularly facilitates workshops designed to bring together emergency planners and the library community to discuss roles and plan partnerships. He has coauthored articles about libraries and emergency planning with his colleague Susan Yowell. Dan earned his master's degree in library science at the State University of New York at Geneseo.

Index

A

AAR (after-action review), 29

"About Foursquare" (Foursquare), 65

active shooter

    Emergency Response Table, 30

    identification of possible hazards, 9

    incident at Virginia Tech, 60

    library planning for, 25

    policy, need for, 2–3

    risk of, 79

    at Texas Medical Center Library, 2–3

    Texas Medical Center Library Active Shooter Checklist, 81

ADR Data Recovery, 123

advance warning risks, 20–25

Aeroscopic Environmental, 123

after-action review (AAR), 29

Aggreko, 123

Agility Recovery Solutions, 123

AIC (American Institute for Conservation of Historic and Artistic Works), 118

Air Quality Sciences, Inc. (AQS), 123

ALA. *See* American Library Association

alert services, 60, 74

Alfred P. Murrah Federal Building, Oklahoma City, 79

American Freeze-Dry Operations, Inc., 123

American Institute for Conservation of Historic and Artistic Works (AIC), 118

American Interfile and Library Services, 124

American Library Association (ALA)

    FEMA policy for libraries as temporary relocation facilities, 91

    link for, services of, 118

    on planning for public health events, 21–22

    preparedness and response resources, 43

American Medical Aid (app), 128

American Psychological Association

    on help from psychologists in crisis, 110, 111

    on responses to disaster/other traumatic event, 112, 113

American Red Cross

    on apps for disaster preparedness and response, 61

    Emergency Social Data Summit, 60

    Facebook survey, 62

    link for, services of, 118

    personal preparedness resources, 70

    role in risk assessment, 8

    Shelter View (app), 128

"America's Most Expensive Natural Disasters" (Woolsey), 20

Americold, 124

"Amerithrax" investigation, 77

AMIA (Association of Moving Image Archivists), 118

Amigos Library Services, 42, 118

ANSUL, 124

anthrax, 77

AP&G (Atlantic Paste and Glue Company), 124

apps

    for disaster preparedness and response, 61

    resources for, 128–131

    for Twitter, 63

APS (Art Preservation Services), 124

AQS (Air Quality Sciences, Inc.), 123

Archival Products, 124

Archivart, 124

Area on Emergency Preparedness and Disaster Relief (website), 115

ARSC (Association for Recorded Sound Collections), 118

Art Preservation Services (APS), 124

assets, inventory of, 13

assistance. *See* outside assistance
Association for Recorded Sound Collections (ARSC), 118
Association of Moving Image Archivists (AMIA), 118
Atlantic Paste and Glue Company (AP&G), 124

B

Bacharach, Inc., 124
backup library
    contact information in SCPReP, 58
    guidelines for setting up, 39, 42
    Memorandum of Understanding Relating to Core Resources and Services Following a Disaster, 40–41
backup system
    identification of critical, 13
    for prevention of loss of connectivity, 38
    setting up, 42
Balboa Art Conservation Center (BACC), 118
Barracuda Networks, 124
Becker, Samantha, 37
BELFOR USA, 12, 44, 124
Bellaire (Texas) Public Library, 93–94
Bengtsson, L., 60–61
biological attacks, 76
Blackmon Mooring Steamatic (BMS), 125
Blackmon-Mooring-Steamatic Catastrophe, Inc. (BMS-CAT), 44
blackouts, 76
Blast, Inc., 125
blogging, 63
bomb threat
    Emergency Response Table, 30
    risk of, 79
    University of Virginia Health Sciences Library Telephone Bomb Threat Checklist, 80
Bougard, Renée, 98
Breighner, Mary, 5
Business Services Manager, 51

C

California State University, 26
campus-wide alerting system, 60
Canadian Association of Professional Conservators (CAPC), 119
Canadian Conservation Institute (CCI), 119
CBL Data Recovery Technologies, Inc., 125
CCAHA (Conservation Center for Art and Historic Artifacts), 119
CDC. *See* Centers for Disease Control and Prevention
Cell On a Light Truck (COLT), 65
Cell On Wheels (COW), 65
cell phone
    for communication after disaster, 73–74

communication plan in SCPReP, 51, 54
    for emergency supply kit, 72
    texting with, 60–61
    tips for communicating before, during, after disasters, 55
    See also mobile technologies
Centers for Disease Control and Prevention (CDC)
    Emergency Preparedness and Response, 116
    Google Flu Trends and, 64
    H1N1 pandemic and, 36–37
    Mobile CDC, 131
    PSAs via text messages, 61
CERT. *See* Community Emergency Response Team
Chan, Margaret, 22
checklists
    disaster restoration partners, checklist for identifying, 10
    Texas Medical Center Library Active Shooter Checklist, 81
    University of Virginia Health Sciences Library Telephone Bomb Threat Checklist, 80
chemical, biological, radiological, and nuclear (CBRN) agents
    anthrax, 77
    national preparedness for, 74
chemical or toxic leaks, 76
CHEMM (Chemical Hazards Emergency Medical Management), 115
Chicora Foundation, Inc., 119
children's resources and services, 96
Christchurch, New Zealand, earthquakes in, 77–78
Chubb Services Corporation, 125
Claude Moore Health Sciences Library at the University of Virginia, 42
Code Blue (Polygon), 12
Cohrs, Mary Alford, 93–94
collection recovery, priority list for, 53, 56
Cologne Archives, Cologne, Germany, 19
COLT (Cell On a Light Truck), 65
Command or Joint Information Center, 95
commercial consultants, 123–127
commercial salvage and recovery companies, 44
communication
    communication plan in SCPReP, 51, 52, 54
    electronics equipment/accessories for emergency supply kit, 72
    for events with little advance warning, 24
    in Hurricane Jenny scenario, 106
    library disaster team roles/contact information in SCPReP, 51
    mobile technologies for disaster preparedness/response, 59–61

in personal preparedness plan, 73–74
    social networking for disaster preparedness/response, 61–63
    tips for communicating before, during, after disasters, 55
community emergency management office, 8
Community Emergency Response Team (CERT)
    librarians as CERT volunteers, 97–98
    role in risk assessment, 8
    training notice, 99
community supporters, librarians as, 95–96
Complete Home First Aid (app), 128
comptroller/accountant, 6
connectivity, 37–38
    See also Internet connectivity
Conney Safety, 125
Conservation Center for Art and Historic Artifacts (CCAHA), 119
conservation centers. *See* library networks/ conservation centers
Conservation Online (CoOL), 116
consultants
    commercial, 123–127
    governmental or organizational, 118–123
contact information
    communication plan in SCPReP, 51, 54
    institutional contacts in SCPReP, 50
    library disaster team roles/contact information in SCPReP, 50–51
    for outside assistance, in SCPReP, 57–58
    in personal preparedness communication plan, 73–74
Continuity of Operations (COOP) plans
    active shooter policy, need for, 2–3
    analysis of current capabilities/hazards, 12
    continuity capability elements of, 1–2
    definition of, 1
    library's role in crisis, 3
    risk assessment, steps in, 5–14
    risk assessment process, 4–5
CoOL (Conservation Online), 116
cooperative engagement
    conclusion about, 112
    earthquakes, Drop, Cover, and Hold On instructions, 108, 109
    food safety during emergency, 107
    Hurricane Jenny scenario, 104–108
    introduction to, 103
    library at high state of readiness, elements of, 105
    Marshall City earthquake scenario, 108–111
    psychologists, support in crisis from, 110, 111
    public health surveillance tools— hurricanes, 104
    responses to disaster/other traumatic event, 112, 113

service continuity planning, ten-step approach, 104
state of emergency, definition of, 106
core services, 15
Cosper-LeBoeuf, Mary, 104
Council of State Archivists (CoSA)
link for, services of, 119
PReP, 12, 49
Council of State Historical Records Coordinators (COSHRC), 119
COW (Cell On Wheels), 65
cross-training, 34–36
Crowdmap, 64
Crowley Company, 125
Curzon, Susan, 26
Cutting Corporation, 125
cyberterrorism, 26

D

Data Retrieval Phoenix, 125
debris flows (lahars), 86–87
denial, 112
Dickerson, Lon, 104
DIMRC (Disaster Information Management Research Center), 109, 119
Director of Collection Management, 51
Director of Information Services, 51
Director of Technology, 51
disaster
library's role in crisis, 3
service interruption, events causing, 4
time to prepare/no time to prepare, 103
Disaster Information Management Research Center (DIMRC), 109, 119
Disaster Mitigation Planning Assistance Website, 116
disaster plan, 17
See also one-page service continuity plan
Disaster Prep (app), 128
disaster preparedness, response, and recovery
mobile technologies for, 59–61
nontraditional roles of librarians after disaster, 96–102
social networking for, 61–63
traditional roles of librarians after disaster, 92–96
Disaster Preparedness for People with Disabilities, 116
disaster restoration partners, checklist for identifying, 10
disaster team, 50–51
DisasterAssistance.gov, 70, 116
disease, 36–37
displaced persons, 94
Document Reprocessors, 125
documentation
for cross-training, 34, 35
for emergency supply kit, 72

Dorlen Products, Inc., 125
drills, 27–29
Duggan, M., 59, 60
DuPont Safety and Protection, 126
Dust Free, 126

E

EAI (Emergency Access Initiative), 43
Earthquake (app), 128
Earthquake Survival Kit (app), 128
earthquakes
in Christchurch, New Zealand, 77–78
Drop, Cover, and Hold On instructions, 108, 109
Emergency Response Table, 30
as event with no warning, 26, 103
impact of Northridge earthquake at California State University, 26
Marshall City earthquake scenario, 108–111
risk of, 76
Eastman Kodak Disaster Recovery Program, 126
ECS (Etherington Conservation Services), 120
educators, librarians as, 96
electronic format, SCPReP available in, 50
electronic medical resources, 94
electronics equipment/accessories, 72
Elmer, S., 65, 66
Emergency Access Initiative (EAI), 43
Emergency Distress Beacon (app), 128
emergency management cycle, 17
Emergency Management Institute (EMI), 119
emergency medical services, 8
Emergency Preparedness and Response (CDC), 70, 116
Emergency Radio (app), 128
emergency response coordinator, 18
emergency response system, 99–100
Emergency Response Table, 30–31
emergency responses. *See* responses, emergency
Emergency Social Data Summit, 60
emergency supply kit
electronics equipment/accessories, 72
first aid supplies, 71
food, 70
infant supplies, 71–72
medications, 71
nose, mouth, skin protection, 71
personal preparedness resources, 70
pet supplies, 73
recommendation for, 69
special needs, 72–73
water, 70
written documents, 72
EMI (Emergency Management Institute), 119

emotions, 112, 113
environmental disasters, 9–10
EPIC Response, 126
equipment
failure, 4
identification of critical, 13
Etherington Conservation Services (ECS), 120
evacuation
of Cologne Archives, 19
Emergency Response Table, 30
evacuees at Houston Public Library post-Katrina, 85–86
family decision about, 74
librarians as information disseminators for evacuees, 94
of special needs persons, 72–73
staff responsibilities for, 18
experts, outside, 8–9
explosion
Emergency Response Table, 30
risk of, 79
external resources, 13
EZ Radar (app), 128

F

face masks, 71
Facebook
apps for alerts/communication, 128
for disaster preparedness and response, 62
for library communication after disaster, 51
"Facebook Key Facts," 62
Facebook Mobile, 62
FaceTime, 54
facilities, identification of critical, 13
Family Emergency Plan (Ready America), 74
Farmer, Sandy, 85–86
FBI (Federal Bureau of Investigation), 77
Featherstone, Robin
on Hurricane Dolly, 20, 21
on librarian roles after disaster, 92
on Northridge earthquake, 26
Federal Bureau of Investigation (FBI), 77
Federal Emergency Management Agency (FEMA)
communication tips for disaster, 54, 55
earthquake safety instructions, 108, 109
emergency services courses from, 33
on ICS training, 100
library as hub for, 95
link for, services of, 120
mitigation as requirement for funding from, 5
NIMS ICS compliance for funding from, 14
policy for libraries as temporary relocation facilities, 91
Public Assistance Program, 91
role in risk assessment, 8

Federal Emergency Management Agency (FEMA) (*cont.*)
  Rumor Control established by, 65
  "whole-community" approach supported by, 60
"15 Elements Demonstrated by a Library at a High State of Readiness" (Wilson), 105
Film Technology Company, Inc., 126
fire
  Emergency Response Table, 30
  identification of possible hazards, for risk assessment, 10
  possible events causing service interruption, 4
  prevention of, 37
  as threat, 79
  at Zimmerman Library, University of New Mexico, 79, 82–83
fire department, 8
first aid supplies, 71
First Choice Drying Equipment Sales and Service, 126
first responders
  CERT training by, 97–98
  library as hub for, 95
  training of by librarian, 96
1st Response: Be Prepared (app), 128
FirstEnergy Corporation, 76
5-0 Radio Pro Police Scanner (app), 129
Flaherty, Grace, 84
flash mobs, 25
flooding
  communication plan in case of, 51
  Emergency Response Table, 30
  identification of possible hazards, for risk assessment, 9–10
  prevention of, 37
  at Renne Library, 26
  at Sidney Memorial Public Library, 84
  as threat, 83
  at University of Iowa Library, 74–76
FloodWatch (app), 129
floor plan, 53, 57
Flu.gov, 116
food
  for emergency supply kit, 70
  food safety during emergency, 107
Forbes.com, 20
Foursquare, 65
Franklin, Benjamin, 36
Fugate, W. Craig, 60
Fukushima, Japan, nuclear accident in, 84, 85

G
Galeras Volcano, Colombia, 87
George R. Brown Convention Center, 85–86
Gerald R. Ford Conservation Center, 120
Getty Conservation Institute (GCI), 120

Ginsberg, J., 64
global positioning system (GPS), 65
GOAT (Generator On A Trailer), 65
Google Flu Trends, 64
Google Mobile, 131
Google Trends, 64
GoToMeeting, 54
governmental consultants, 118–123
GPS (global positioning system), 65
Guttenfelder, David, 84, 85

H
H1N1 influenza ("swine flu") pandemic
  library backup system for staff illness, 42
  library preparation for prevention of, 21, 36–37
  in post-pandemic period, 22
Haiti, earthquake in, 60–61
Halotron, Inc., 126
Halsted, Deborah
  on active shooter policy, 2–3
  on ICS training, 100
  on JIC drill skills, 101
Hamilton, Rebecca, 104
Hardin Library of the Health Sciences at the University of Iowa, 38, 39
Harman, Wendy, 60
hashtag, 63
hazardous materials spill, 30
hazards
  identification of possible, for risk assessment, 9–10
  in vulnerability analysis, 10–12
  See also risks; threats
Health Hotlines (app), 129
Health Sciences Library at the University of North Carolina in Chapel Hill, 42
help. *See* outside assistance
"Helping United States Libraries After Disasters" (American Library Association), 44
Here I Am (app), 129
Heritage Preservation, 120
high priority rescue order list, 53, 57
Homeland Security, 34
hostage, 31
Huang, Gloria, 60
human events, 4
human hazards, 9–10
human impact, 11
human resources (HR) representative, 7
Humane Society Disaster Planning for Pets, 116
Hurricane Dolly, 20, 21
Hurricane Ike
  Bellaire (Texas) Public Library recovery efforts from, 93–94
  library services after, 7

public library card registration after, 92
  Texas Medical Center Library's electrical facilities and, 14
Hurricane Irene, 64
Hurricane Jenny scenario, 104–108
Hurricane Katrina
  emergency print medical resources for evacuees, 94
  Houston Public Library after, 85–86
  library services after, 3
Hurricane Pro (app), 129
Hurricane Sandy, 65
hurricanes/typhoons
  Houston Public Library post-Katrina, 85–86
  Hurricane Jenny scenario, 104–108
  hurricane preparedness on YouTube, 63
  planning for events with advance warning, 20–21
  public health surveillance tools, 104
  special needs evacuation assistance, 73
  as threat, 84–85
  time to prepare for, 103

I
ICA (Intermuseum Conservation Association), 120
ICE (In Case of Emergency) contacts
  in personal preparedness communication plan, 73–74
  tips for communicating before, during, after disasters, 55
ICEcare (app), 129
ICS (Incident Command System), 99–100
ICS (Industrial Cold Storage), 126
iFeltThat (app), 129
iFirstAid (app), 129
iGetThru (app), 129
III (Insurance Information Institute), 120
ILL (interlibrary loan), 42
ILLiad, 42
illness
  library backup system for staff illness, 42
  prevention of, 36–37
Image Permanence Institute (IPI), 120
immediate responses, 18–19
impact
  of emergency, in vulnerability analysis, 11
  in risk assessment, 5
Incident Command System (ICS), 99–100
Industrial Cold Storage (ICS), 126
infant supplies, 71–72
influenza (flu), 86
  See also H1N1 influenza ("swine flu") pandemic
information community builders, librarians as, 96
information disseminators, librarians as, 94

information gathering/dissemination, 101–102

information technology (IT) director, 6–7

Insects Limited, Inc., 126

institutional contacts, 50, 52

institutional supporters, librarians as, 95

insurance, inventory of assets for, 13

insurance assessment, 13–14

Insurance Information Institute (III), 120

interlibrary loan (ILL), 42

Intermuseum Conservation Association (ICA), 120

internal resources, 13

Internet connectivity
    library Internet access, use of, 37
    prevention of loss of, 37–38
    service continuity plan in SCPReP, 54
    smartphone use for, 59–60

inventory, of library assets, 13

Iowa, flooding in, 74–76

IPI (Image Permanence Institute), 120

iSOS Alert (app), 129

iSurvive (app), 129

Ivins, Bruce, 77

J

Japan, nuclear accident in Fukushima, 84, 85

Jive Media, 61

Johnston, Lauren, 63

Joint Information Center (JIC), 101

Joint Information System (JIS), 101–102

Joplin, Missouri, 87–89

Journal of the Medical Library Association, 92

K

Kaine, Timothy, 60

Kidde-Fenwall, 126

Kraft, Nancy, 74–76

Krums, Janis, 63

L

lahars (debris flows), 86–87

Lambert, Toni, 85

landslides
    description of, 86
    USGS National Landslide Hazards Program, 84

Lawrence, Janna, 38, 39

Levs, Josh, 61

librarians
    as CERT volunteers, 97–98
    Incident Command System training, 100
    nontraditional roles after disaster, 96–102
    traditional roles after disaster, 92–96
    willingness to help community after disaster, 91–92

library
    Bellaire (Texas) Public Library recovery efforts from Hurricane Ike, 93–94
    earthquake response of Central Library, University of Canterbury, 77–78
    fire at Zimmerman Library, University of New Mexico, 79, 82–83
    flooding at Sidney Memorial Public Library, 84
    at high state of readiness, elements of, 105
    Houston Public Library post-Katrina, 85–86
    hurricane scenario for cooperative engagement, 104–108
    pandemic preparedness planning, 21–24
    as temporary relocation facility, 91
    University of Iowa Main Library, response to flooding, 74–76

library director, 6, 51

library disaster team, in SCPReP, 50–52

library networks/conservation centers
    American Library Association, 43
    Amigos Library Services, 42
    contact information in SCPReP, 58
    Emergency Access Initiative, 43
    LYRASIS, 43
    National Network of Libraries of Medicine, 43
    NN/LM EP&R Toolkit, 43
    Northeast Document Conservation Center, 43
    WESTPAS, 43

Library of Congress (LC) Preservation Directorate, 121

library services, identification of critical, 12

library staff. *See* staff

licensing, 39

Life360 (app), 130

little advance warning risks
    categorization of, 20
    planning for events with little advance warning, 24–25

losses, estimation of possible, 13

Lurie, N., 65, 66

Lyon, Becky J., 92

LYRASIS, 43, 121

M

MACC (Midwest Art Conservation Center), 121

management by objective, 99

Mario E. Ramirez, M.D. Library, 20, 21

Maron, Dina Fine, 65–66

Marrone, Matt, 63

Marshall City earthquake scenario, 108–111

mayor/community administrator, 8

MBK Consulting, 127

McKnight, Michelynn, 91–92

McKnight, Sue, 77–78

medical emergency, 31

medical resources, 94

medications, 71

MedlinePlus
    link for, description of, 116
    mobile-optimized website, 131
    personal preparedness resources, 70

Memorial Institute for the Prevention of Terrorism (MIPT), Lawson Library, 116

Menster, Kari, 10

Merchant, R. M., 65, 66

Merck Manual of Diagnosis and Therapy, 94

microblogging, 63

Middletown Public Library, Pennsylvania, 51

Midwest Art Conservation Center (MACC), 121

Midwest Freeze Dry, Ltd., 127

Miller, Michael J., 65

Minkel, J. R., 76

Minnesota Historical Society Salvage Procedures for Wet Items, 116

mitigation
    consideration of options, 14
    as element of emergency management cycle, 17
    in risk assessment process, 5

mobile access, SCPReP, 50, 54

Mobile CDC, 131

mobile devices
    communication plan in SCPReP, 51, 54
    tips for communicating before, during, after disasters, 55

mobile technologies
    adoption of, 59
    apps, 61
    availability/use of, 59–60
    challenges of use for disaster preparedness/response, 65–66
    Facebook access via, 62
    mobile infrastructure challenges, 65
    texting, 60–61
    YouTube access via, 63

mobile technologies resources
    apps, 128–131
    mobile-optimized websites, 131

Mobile.twitter.com, 63

mobs, 25

model memorandum of understanding (MOU)
    for backup library plan, 39
    example of, 40–41

Moody Medical Library of the University of Texas Medical Branch in Galveston, 7

Mount Etna, Italy, 87

Mount Ranier, 86–87

Mount St. Helens eruption, 86, 87
mouth protection, 71

N

"Narratives from the Storm" (*Texas Library Journal*), 3
National Archives Preservation Programs, 121
National Center for Animal Health Emergency Management (NCAHEM), 121
National Emergency Management Association (NEMA), 121
National Emergency Preparedness and Response Initiative
  of NN/LM, 43
  pandemic preparedness table, 22–23
National Fire Protection Association (NFPA), 122
National Flood Insurance Program (NFIP), 122
National Hurricane Center (NHC)
  link for, services of, 122
  YouTube videos on hurricane preparedness, 63
National Incident Management System (NIMS)
  function of, 33
  Incident Command System, 99–100
  Joint Information System, 101–102
  link for, services of, 116
National Library of Medicine
  list of medical books for emergencies, 109
  NN/LM, 43
  risk assessment information in TOXNET, 4
  Special Populations: Emergency and Disaster Preparedness, 117
  Specialized Information Services, 117
National Network of Libraries of Medicine (NN/LM)
  contact information in SCPReP, 57
  description of, 43
  Emergency Preparedness and Response Toolkit, 43, 117
  pandemic preparedness table, 22–23
National Response Framework (NRF), 33, 34
National Voluntary Organization Active in a Disaster (National VOAD), 122
National Weather Service (NWS)
  Facebook postings by, 62
  link for, description of, 117
  mobile-optimized website, 131
  personal preparedness resources, 70
  role in risk assessment, 9
  tornado warnings, 24
natural disasters
  planning for events with advance warning, 20–21

planning for events with little advance warning, 24–25
planning for events with no warning, 26
possible events causing service interruption, 4
See also threats
NCAHEM (National Center for Animal Health Emergency Management), 121
NEDCC (Northeast Document Conservation Center), 43, 122
neighboring institutions, 9
NEMA (National Emergency Management Association), 121
Nevado del Ruiz volcano, Colombia, 86
New England Journal of Medicine, 65
New Jersey Hospital Association, 39, 40–41
New Jersey Office of Emergency Management, 106
New Pig, 127
New Zealand, earthquakes in Christchurch, 77–78
NFIP (National Flood Insurance Program), 122
NFPA (National Fire Protection Association), 122
NHC (National Hurricane Center), 63, 122
NIMS. *See* National Incident Management System
911 Police Radio (app), 130
NN/LM. *See* National Network of Libraries of Medicine
no warning risks
  categorization of, 20
  planning for events with no warning, 26
Northeast Document Conservation Center (NEDCC), 43, 122
nose protection, 71
NRF (National Response Framework), 33, 34
nuclear threats
  CBRN agents, national preparedness for, 74
  description of, 86
  nuclear accident in Fukushima, 84, 85
  Radiation Emergency Medical Management app, 130
NWS. *See* National Weather Service

O

off-site planning, 33, 38
Ohio, power outage in, 76
Old Dominion University, Norfolk, Virginia, 25
one-page service continuity plan
  back side of SCPReP, 53
  background, 49
  communication plan, 51, 54
  communication tips for before, during, after disasters, 55
  floor plans, 57
  front side of SCPReP, 52

getting help, 57–58
high priority rescue order list, 57
institutional contacts, 50
library disaster team roles/contact information, 50–51
mobile SCPReP, 54
priority recovery list/vendor contacts, 56–57
scenario to illustrate value of, 47–49
SCPReP with prepaid phone card, 54
service continuity plan, 54
Service Continuity Pocket Response Plan, 50
service continuity team, 56
one-person plan, 34–36
on-site planning
  cross-training, 34–36
  knowledge of, 33
  prevention, 36–38
ooVoo, 54
Opportunity for All: How the American Public Benefits from Internet Access at Public Libraries (Becker et al.), 37
organization, flexible/modular, 99
organizational capabilities, 13
organizational consultants, 118–123
Orkin, 127
Outbreaks Near Me (app), 130
outside assistance
  backup library, 39, 42
  commercial salvage and recovery companies, 44
  contact information for, in SCPReP, 57–58
  knowledge of, 33
  for library, need for, 34
  library networks/conservation centers, 42–44
  Memorandum of Understanding Relating to Core Resources and Services Following a Disaster, 40–41
outside experts, 8–9

P

Page, Julie, 127
Pan American Health Organization (PAHO) Area on Emergency Preparedness and Disaster Relief, 122
pandemics
  pandemic flu history, 1918–1919, 86
  pandemic planning table, 22–23
  planning for, 21–22, 24
  prevention of illness, library strategies for, 36–37
personal preparedness
  basic emergency supply kit, 69–73
  importance of, 69
  plan, creation of, 73–74
  plan for library staff, 92
personal property, 14

Pest Control Services, Inc., 127
pet supplies, 73
Pettinger, Anne, 26
Pew Research Center's Internet and
    American Life Project, 59–60
Peyton, William, 5
Physicians' Desk Reference, 94
Pillbox (app), 130
Pisano-Pedigo, Lynn, 60
planning
    communication plan in SCPReP, 51, 54
    for events with advance warning, 20–22,
        24
    for events with little advance warning,
        24–25
    for events with no warning, 26
    off-site planning, 38
    outside assistance, 39–44
    pandemic planning table, 22–23
    personal preparedness plan, 69, 73–74
    service continuity planning, ten-step
        approach, 104
    on-site planning, 34–38
    See also Continuity of Operations
        (COOP) plans; one-page service
        continuity plan
planning commission, 9
Pocket First Aid and CPR (app), 61, 130
Pocket Response Plan (PReP), 12
police department, role in risk assessment, 8
Polygon, 127
power outage
    backup power plan for Internet access, 38
    cyberterrorism, planning for, 26
    documentation redundancy for, 34
    Emergency Response Table, 31
    emergency supply kit and, 70, 72
    in northeast, 76
PReP (Pocket Response Plan), 12
prepaid phone card, 54
preparedness, 17
    See also personal preparedness
preservationist, 57
prevention
    of fire, 37
    of flooding/water leaks, 37
    of illness, 36–37
    of loss of connectivity, 37–38
print resources
    removal of in preparation for hurricane,
        20, 21
    salvage and recovery companies for print
        collection, 44
priority items
    identification of for salvage plan, 13
    priority list for collection recovery in
        SCPReP, 53, 56
procedures, for one-person plan for library
    services, 34–36

property impact, 11
property manager/head of facilities, 6
ProTEXT, 127
psychologists, 110, 111
PTSD Coach (app), 130
Public Health Emergency, 117
public health events
    pandemic planning table, 22–23
    planning for events with advance
        warning, 21–22, 24
Public Health—Seattle and King County
    Meeting the Needs of Vulnerable
    Populations/Equity in Emergency
    Response, 117
public health surveillance tools, 104
public information, Joint Information
    System, 101–102
public service announcements (PSAs)
    CDC PSAs via text messages, 61
    YouTube videos on hurricane
        preparedness, 63
public works department, 8
PubMed Mobile, 131
pyroclastic surges, 87

R

Rackspace, 127
Radiation Emergency Medical Management
    (REMM) (app), 130
RAP (Regional Alliance for Preservation),
    122
Ready America, 74
Ready.gov, 70, 117
real property, definition of, 14
recovery
    Bellaire (Texas) Public Library recovery
        efforts from Hurricane Ike, 93–94
    as element of emergency management
        cycle, 17
    from fire at Zimmerman Library,
        University of New Mexico, 79, 82–83
redundancy, 54
Reed, Jack, 91
reference services, 39
Regional Alliance for Preservation (RAP),
    122
Reliable Automatic Sprinkler Company, Inc.,
    127
Relief Central (app), 130
remote library sites, 38
Renne Library, Montana State University, 26
reporting structure, 29
Rerat, Cari, 87–89
resources
    consultants, 118–127
    identification of in analysis of current
        capabilities/hazards, 13
    internal/external, in vulnerability analysis,
        11, 12

mobile technologies, 128–131
    personal preparedness resources, 70
    websites, 115–117
responses, emergency
    after-action review, 29
    conclusion about, 29
    drills to assist in training for response,
        27–29
    emergency management cycle, 17
    Emergency Response Table, 30–31
    immediate responses, importance of,
        18–19
    pandemic planning table, 22–23
    planning for events with advance
        warning, 20–22, 24
    planning for events with little advance
        warning, 24–25
    planning for events with no warning, 26
    potential risks, categories of, 20
ReUnite (app), 130
review, of risk assessment, 14
Reyna, Greysi, 20, 21
riots, 25
risk assessment
    as first step in COOP, 2–3
    process, 4–5
    steps in, 5–14
risk assessment planning team, 5–9
risk assessment steps
    conclusion about, 15
    hazards, identification of possible, 9–10
    insurance assessment, 13–14
    inventory assets, estimate possible losses,
        13
    mitigation options, 14
    outside experts, 8–9
    review/update, 14
    risk assessment planning team, creation
        of, 5–7
    strengths/weaknesses, analysis of, 12–13
    vulnerability analysis, 10–12
risks
    pandemic planning table, 22–23
    planning for events with advance
        warning, 20–22, 24
    planning for events with little advance
        warning, 24–25
    planning for events with no warning, 26
    potential risks, categories of, 20
    See also threats
RSOE EDIS, 117
Ruffin, Angela B., 92

S

safety manager, 6
salvage and recovery companies
    contact information in SCPReP, 58
    list of, 44
sarin, 76

Scientific American, 65
SCPReP. *See* Service Continuity PReP
self-sufficiency, 33
Send.Morse (app), 130
service continuity plan
    in Hurricane Jenny scenario, 105–106
    in SCPReP, elements of, 54
    ten-step approach to, 104
Service Continuity PReP (SCPReP)
    back side of, 53
    background, 49
    communication plan, 51, 54
    communication tips for before, during,
        after disasters, 55
    floor plans, 57
    front side of, 52
    getting help, 57–58
    high priority rescue order list, 57
    institutional contacts, 50
    library disaster team roles/contact
        information, 50–51
    mobile SCPReP, 54
    with prepaid phone card, 54
    priority recovery list/vendor contacts,
        56–57
    scenario to illustrate value of, 47–48
    service continuity plan, 54
    service continuity team, 56
service continuity team, 52, 56
service disruptions
    off-site planning, 38
    outside assistance, 39–44
    possible events causing, 4
    prevention strategies to minimize,
        36–38
service impact, 11
Sheketoff, Emily, 91
shock, 112
shooter. *See* active shooter
short message service (SMS), 60–61
Sidney Memorial Public Library, Sidney,
    New York, 84
skin protection, 71
Skype, 54
smart-ICE (In Case of Emergency) (app), 130
smartphones
    apps for disaster preparedness and
        response, 61
    availability/use of, 59–60
    Foursquare with, 65
    See also cell phone
Smith, A., 59
SMS (short message service), 60–61
social networking
    challenges of use for disaster
        preparedness/response, 65–66
    for disaster preparedness and response,
        59, 61–62
    Facebook, 62

for library communication after disaster,
    51
    National Weather Service posting
        information, 62
    Twitter, 63
    YouTube, 62–63
SOS! Emergency Preparedness (app), 131
Spanish Flu, 86
span-of-control, 100
Special Libraries Association, 88, 89
special needs, 72–73
staff
    analysis of current strengths/weaknesses,
        12
    cross-training and, 34–36
    emergency response responsibilities,
        18–19
    HR representative on risk assessment
        planning team, 7
    identification of critical, 13
    library backup system for staff illness, 42
    library disaster team roles/contact
        information in SCPReP, 50–51
    off-site planning and, 38
    pandemic preparedness planning,
        21–22
    personal preparedness plan for, 69
    prevention of illness and, 36–37
Stafford Act, 91
state library, 57
"State Library of Louisiana and Public
    Libraries' Response to Hurricanes:
    Lessons, Issues and Strategies"
    (Hamilton), 104
state of emergency, 106
strengths, 12–13
Su, Y. S., 64
Sumter Regional Hospital, Americus,
    Georgia, 19
SwiftRiver, 64–65
swine flu. *See* H1N1 influenza ("swine flu")
    pandemic

T
tabletop exercise (TTE), 27–29
Talmadge, Eric, 84, 85
team
    library disaster team roles/contact
        information in SCPReP, 50–51
    risk assessment planning team, creation
        of, 5–9
    service continuity team, 52, 56
telecommuting, 38
telephone. *See* cell phone; smartphones
telephone company, 9
temporary relocation facilities, libraries as,
    91
"10-Step Approach to Service Continuity
    Planning" (Wilson), 105

tephra (ash and coarser debris), 87
terminology, universal, 99
terrorism, acts of
    anthrax, 77
    cyberterrorism, planning for, 26
    possible events causing service
        interruption, 4
Texas, Hurricane Dolly in, 20, 21
Texas Department of State Health Services,
    104
Texas Library Journal, 3
Texas Medical Center Library, Houston,
    Texas
    active shooter at, 2–3
    Active Shooter Checklist, 81
    electrical facilities moved in, 14
    ICS training for librarians, 100
    JIC drill skills, 101
    library services after Hurricane Ike, 7
text messaging
    CDC PSAs, 61
    for communication after disaster, 73–74
    for disaster preparedness and response,
        60–61
Thompson, Marty, 18–19
Thorkildsen, Z., 64
threats
    biological attacks, 76
    blackouts, 76
    chemical or toxic leaks, 76
    earthquakes, 76–78
    explosions, bomb threats, active shooters,
        79
    fire at Zimmerman Library, University of
        New Mexico, 79, 82–83
    fires, 79
    flooding, 83–84
    hurricanes/typhoons, 84–86
    Iowa flooding, 74–76
    landslide hazards program, USGS, 84
    landslides, 86
    nuclear accident in Fukushima, Japan,
        84, 85
    nuclear threats, 86
    pandemic flu history, 1918–1919, 86
    pandemics, 86–87
    power outage in northeast, 76
    SLA in tsunami relief effort, 88, 89
    Texas Medical Center Library Active
        Shooter Checklist, 81
    tornadoes, 87–89
    tsunamis, 89
    University of Virginia Health Sciences
        Library Telephone Bomb Threat
        Checklist, 80
    volcanic eruptions, hazards associated
        with, 86, 87
    volcanoes, 89
    See also risks

tornadoes
  destruction of Sumter Regional Hospital, Americus, Georgia, 19
  Emergency Response Table, 31
  Joplin (MO) tornado, 87–89
  planning for, 24–25
  as threat, 87
Trabish, Herman K., 26
training
  CERT training, 97–98
  cross-training, 34–36
  drills to assist in training for response, 27–29
  Incident Command System training, 100
  librarians as trainers, 96
  special skills training, 99
traumatic event, responses to, 112, 113
tsunamis
  description of, 89
  nuclear accident in Fukushima, 84, 85
  Special Libraries Association in tsunami relief effort, 88, 89
TTE (tabletop exercise), 27–29
Tweetdeck (app), 63
Twitpic (app), 63
Twitter
  crisis information on, 63
  for disaster preparedness and response, 63
  for library communication after disaster, 51
  link for, 131
211.org
  link for, services of, 117
  personal preparedness resources, 70
  for special needs evacuation assistance, 73
typhoons. See hurricanes/typhoons

U

United Way, 72, 73
unity of command, 99
universal terminology, 99
University of Canterbury Central Library, 77–78
University of Iowa Library, 74–76
University of New Mexico Zimmerman Library, 79, 82–83
University of Texas, shooting at, 2–3, 79
University of Virginia Claude Moore Health Sciences Library
  Emergency Response Table used at, 29
  one-person plan for library services, 35–36

response to tornado warning, 24–25
University of Virginia Health Sciences Library Telephone Bomb Threat Checklist, 80
update
  of disaster plan, 49
  library as location for updates, 95
  of risk assessment, 14
U.S. Airways Flight 1549, 63
U.S. Department of Agriculture Food Safety and Inspection Service, 107
U.S. Department of Health and Human Services (HHS), 74
U.S. Department of Homeland Security, 74
U.S. Environmental Protection Agency, 4–5
U.S. Food and Drug Administration, 5
U.S. Geological Survey (USGS), 84
U.S. Government Accountability Office, 74
USA.gov, 117
user-generated data
  challenges of use for disaster preparedness/response, 65–66
  Foursquare, 65
  Google Trends/Google Flu Trends, 64
  Ushahidi, 64–65
Ushahidi, 64–65
USHospFinder (app), 131
utilities, 9

V

Vancouver, Canada, 25
vendor contacts, 56–57
Verizon, 65
video, YouTube, 62–63
video calling, 54
video conferencing, 54
Virginia Tech, shooting incident at, 60, 79
Virtual Operations Support Teams (VOSTs), 66
volcanoes
  description of, 89
  hazards associated with volcanic eruptions, 86–87
vulnerability analysis, 10–12

W

WADEM (World Association for Disaster and Emergency Management), 123
Wardell, C., 64
water, for emergency supply kit, 70
water leaks, prevention of, 37
weaknesses, 12–13

weather, severe, 31
Weather Alert USA (app), 131
Weather Channel, 117
weather-related events, 20–21
WebEx, 54
website resources
  mobile-optimized websites, 131
  resources for disaster planning/recovery, 115–117
West Lake Conservators, 122
West Pittston Public Library, 51
Western States and Territories Preservation Assistance Service (WESTPAS), 43, 123
White, Bill, 85
"whole-community" approach, 60
Wilkinson, Fran, 79, 82–83
Wilson, Daniel T.
  on backup system, 42
  on Hurricane Dolly, 20, 21
  on impact of Northridge earthquake, 26
  library at high state of readiness, elements of, 105
Wireless Information System for Emergency Responders (WISER), 96, 131
Wisconsin Department of Public Instruction, 21
Woolley, Dan, 61
Woolsey, Matt, 20
Woolsey, R. James, 26
World Association for Disaster and Emergency Management (WADEM), 123
World Health Organization (WHO), 22

Y

Young, J. Chris, 7
YouTube, 62–63
YouTube for Mobile, 131
Yowell, Susan
  one-person plan for library services, 35–36
  on response to tornado warning, 24–25

Z

Zach, Lisl, 91–92
Zimmerman Library, University of New Mexico, 79, 82–83